EMP ATTACK

Crucial Lessons on How to Survive the Most Overlooked Disaster the World

(Surviving a Catastrophic Emp Attack That Brings Down the National Power Grid)

Mark Gibbs

Published By Mark Gibbs

Mark Gibbs

All Rights Reserved

Emp Attack: Crucial Lessons on How to Survive the Most Overlooked Disaster the World (Surviving a Catastrophic Emp Attack That Brings Down the National Power Grid)

ISBN 978-1-77485-419-8

All rights reserved. No part of this guide may be reproduced in any form without permission in writing from the publisher except in the case of brief quotations embodied in critical articles or reviews.

Legal & Disclaimer

The information contained in this book is not designed to replace or take the place of any form of medicine or professional medical advice. The information in this book has been provided for educational and entertainment purposes only.

The information contained in this book has been compiled from sources deemed reliable, and it is accurate to the best of the Author's knowledge; however, the Author cannot guarantee its accuracy and validity and cannot be held liable for any errors or omissions. Changes are periodically made to this book. You must consult your doctor or get professional medical advice before using any of the suggested remedies, techniques, or information in this book.

Upon using the information contained in this book, you agree to hold harmless the Author from and against any damages, costs, and expenses, including any legal fees potentially resulting from the application of any of the information provided by this guide. This disclaimer applies to any damages or injury caused by the use and application, whether directly or indirectly, of any advice or information presented, whether for breach of contract, tort, negligence, personal injury, criminal intent, or under any other cause of action.

You agree to accept all risks of using the information presented inside this book. You need to consult a professional medical practitioner in order to ensure you are both able and healthy enough to participate in this program.

TABLE OF CONTENTS

INTRODUCTION 1

CHAPTER 1: WHAT COULD BE THE CAUSE OF A GRID-DOWN 3

CHAPTER 2: WHAT WOULD AN EMP-RELATED ATTACK LOOK LIKE? 8

CHAPTER 3: ARE EMP AN ACTUAL THREAT? AND BY WHOM? 11

CHAPTER 4: PREPARING FOR UNEXPECTED BLACKOUTS . 25

CHAPTER 5: HOME PREPARATION 36

CHAPTER 6: BASIC URBAN SURVIVAL SKILLS.................... 42

CHAPTER 7: FOOD AND WATER 62

CHAPTER 8: THE MOST IMPORTANT TYPES OF GUNS TO INCLUDE IN YOUR ARMORY 77

CHAPTER 9: THE TOP 10 EMP FAULTS TO AVOID 95

CHAPTER 10: HYDRATION PACKS 120

CHAPTER 11: WATER 130

CHAPTER 12: COOKING, COOLING, HEATING AND LIGHTING.. 135

CHAPTER 13: WHAT DEFENSE IS THERE AGAINST EMP? 143

CHAPTER 14: FINDING AN EMERGENCY HEATING SOURCE 149

CHAPTER 15: WHAT'S WHAT IS AN EMP ATTACK?......... 155

CHAPTER 16: SOLAR PANELS THE MOST EFFECTIVE TYPES TO MAKE 163

CONCLUSION 182

Introduction

Have you ever thought that in one moment, the world like we live it may be thrown back to our Stone Age? Imagine a world in which commercial airliners disappear from the sky, in which all power is cut off and motorized transportation no longer operates, where all communications are gone, the backup power source is almost absent, and in which 90% of America's population dies within the first few months.

Perhaps worse...imagine this happening for a few months, perhaps even years. The scenario being presented to you could be consequence from the occurrence of an EMP (electromagnetic pulse) attack. The power grid in the United States is extremely fragile and an attack that is successful could result in the worst threat ever recorded in our history. In reality, it is difficult to consider"the" United States a 'nation' following the event of an EMP attack.

Through this guide, you'll learn you can live in an environment that is not ruled by power. Many millions of Americans are worried about the likelihood of an attack and have taken necessary steps in preparing to safeguard themselves as well as their loved ones. Today, you have the chance to be one of them.

Let's get started:

Chapter 1: What Could Be The Cause Of A Grid-Down

and The Value Of Being Ready

Are you still skeptical of the possibility that a grid might fail? There are a variety of scenarios that could lead to an electrical grid malfunction. A major breakdown could cause an effect of trickle-down that could lead to a malfunction in the system for water distribution. Natural gas lines can be damaged, rendering the entire country in a state of utter suffocation and frozen for those who depend on gas to power the furnace of their home.

The following are the most probable causes of an extensive grid failure:

A nuclear weapon doesn't just pose a threat to the health of humans. In fact the nuclear weapon does not even need to be exploded close to the surface of the earth in order to cause major harm. A small nuclear weapon that was able to explode in the atmosphere of Earth could cause an electromagnetic pulse that could disrupt the electrical grid. One blast could wipe away half of the nation in just a few seconds.

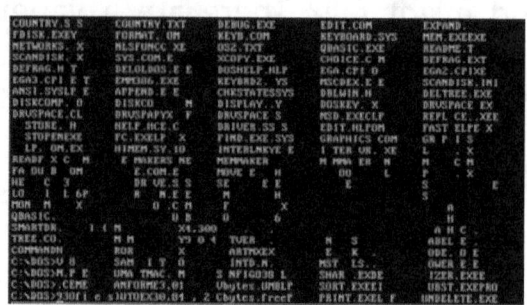

- A hacker on computers or a well-executed virus could damage the electricity grid. It is a likely scenario and could cause damage to the entire system across the nation. The risk of the virus infiltrating the power system is just part of the fight. A virus could cause disruption to our communication and banking systems as well as transportation systems. The scenario has already occurred in a smaller amount. This could be an introduction to the future.

* Solar flares could release an electromagnetic signal (EMP) which could destroy power systems. There are hundreds of flares that occur every each day. These flares are relatively tiny and do not cause any significant difficulties. There have been massive solar flares in the past which disrupted satellite systems, however, even those were small when compared to the damage the sun can create. One scientist thinks the risk of a huge solar flares is greater than the possibility of a nuclear bomb that causes the same-sized EMP.

* An attack that physically targets multiple power stations at the same time can also cause havoc on the power grid. This has happened however on a very small scale. In the event that a concerted attack were initiated, it could result in an extensive grid failure. The damage could be catastrophic and may take several months after where it will be able to recover.

Above: The Fukushima nuclear disaster of 2011 is probably the most well known incident where natural disaster caused a major grid failure

A natural disaster which knocks out the electricity grid is a possibility. Take a look back at the Fukushima catastrophe. A seismic event caused an array of events that caused cataclysmic damage.

These are only a few possibilities that might take place. It doesn't take a conspiracy theorist in order to hold these thoughts. It's not difficult to plan for this type of situation. Making the effort to prepare today can save your family's life tomorrow.

Chapter 2: What Would An Emp-Related Attack Look Like?

You're probably thinking, "what does an EMP mean to me?"

This chapter we'll look at the immediate, short-term and long-term consequences that could result from EMP attacks. EMP strike on your as well as the world around you.

The immediate effects from EMP Attacks:
EMP Attack:

These are some of the first consequences of an EMP attack could be able to have on the world around you

The lights will go outand your surroundings will turn into darkness

- All electronic devices stop functioning and stop immediately.

Trains can get stuck or completely derail
- All public transportation will be stopped
Planes will drop out from the sky
Electronic components inside automobiles will fail which causes cars to stall and smash into each other in the roadway

Elevators could get trapped, trapping hundreds of thousands, if not instantly millions.

The Short-Term Impacts from an EMP Attack

Here are the short-term consequences that can be expected from an EMP attack that will take place immediately after the immediate effects that we have described:

Uncontrolled fires could destroy all of the United States as a result of automobile accident, transformers that explode and planes crashing out from the sky and falling into the ground

Water is not able to stop these fires as the water pumps need electricity

The entire ATM machines as well as banks inactive, which means you won't be able to be able to access your funds at the bank
- Gas stations, stores and restaurants will be shut down

If there isn't enough refrigeration food items, they will begin to deteriorate

You won't have access to the basic water and utilities

Long-term effects of the EMP Attack

Then, here are the long-term consequences that can be a result of having an EMP attack:
- People will start turning to one another to procure the desperately needed items as the water and food supply diminishes

People who have been who are trapped by the EMP attack are likely to die from starvation, or dehydration.

Looting and rioting will be a common sight in urban zones

Mass violence is expected to erupt all across the United States

The economy will fall apart and the paper currency will be worthless

The world will gradually but steadily become chaotic as there aren't enough police officers to maintain the peace

Once you know the exact nature of an EMP attack is and feel like in following section we will go over exactly what you should do if an EMP attack takes place.

Chapter 3: Are Emp An Actual Threat? And By Whom?

North Korea has been threatening to "incinerate" the United States for several years in the past. Then, it appears that U.S. has a President who seems to be fighting the fire with fire, taking the time to tell the United Nations that if the U.S. is provoked, North Korea will be "destroyed" The danger from N.K. appears to be the most significant. It is true that North Korea appears to be the most likely target. North Korea is certainly not the only country to shock Western Civilization by turning the lights off by the power of an EMP blast. There are many actors who could be responsible for such an attack. In this chapter, we'll discuss some of the most plausible scenarios.

Surprising Attacks by Russia

A lot of people have poked at those who express any issue related to conflict between United States and the former Soviet Union. However, even though it is true that the Cold War is long over and we live in a an extremely new world today, it is that United States and Russia are the two largest militaries on earth and even if these two countries are best of friends in the present (contrary to what the majority of thinkers in the field of policy think) it won't take long for the relationship to degrade.

In addition the Russians are believed to have the most sophisticated EMP program ever created. If push came to push, there's certainty that the Kremlin has plans for contingency to deploy EMP to attack its adversaries, the United States. In the event that Russia thought that nuclear confrontation between America was imminent, for instance. United States was imminent for instance, the most popular theory is that the Russian leadership would seek to escape the consequences that comes with "mutually certain destruction" through launching such massive EMP in which the U.S. would be knocked out before it could launch even a single nuclear missile.

In order for this to happen in the first place, the Russians will need to have a very powerful and precise EMP weapon as well as to have a lot of luck in order to produce an electro magnetic storm, which would ensure that would ensure that the U.S. is blacked out from coast to coast (they must also be hopeful the U.S. nuclear subs wouldn't be able reach the area before they were disabled by the electrical pulse). The odds of such a catastrophe for America could seem like a fantasy yet even the slightest chance of an outcome being negative must be considered.

Chinese Retaliatory Strike

Even in the most rosy of times , the United States and China have an extremely tense relationship. There are a variety of ways in which the U.S. and China can clash in a negative way, leading to a devastating military conflict. One thing is that -- and as you'll observe is a frequent theme throughout this book--China is in a loose alliance to North Korea, and in the wake of recent threats posed at North Korea to the United States the possibility exists that a conflict will occur that draws China in with it.

How could such the worst-case scenario play out? Absolutely given the current stance the leader Kim Jong Un of Korea has taken. The leader. Kim has been persistently challenging the boundaries that the United States and the rest of the world are able to accept. The world is fast realizing that if they advise Kim. Kim not to do something, in defiance and rage, the Korean leader will go ahead with it. The government told him that he should not launch rockets in the Sea of Japan, so the missiles are launched quickly the next day.

Then, after making threats to attack Guam, the U.S. defense outpost in Guam located in middle of Pacific Ocean, Mr. Kim was warned by the military by the military to "not ever think of the idea". What then does Kim. Kim do? The next day, he informs the world press that he's not planning to directly strike Guam, but that's crazy! But he would prefer to launch a massive nuclear bomb just in the middle of the ocean instead!

The sexy head of North Korea is literally testing the waters by pushing and pushing inch by inch to determine how far he is able to take things.

Should North Korea did drop a nuclear bomb on the shores of Guam even though it might not cause direct injuries it is clear that it would be a huge risk to the United States could not (without totally losing face and losing any credibility) remain silent and let North Korea get away with the explosion of nuclear bombs just out of the harbor! In the event that they allowed it, the U.S. allowed this they should be able to permit anything. If it happens that the U.S. does respond to this threatening act The shrewd North Korean leader could rightfully claim they've proved that the nuclear explosion off the coasts of Guam did not technically harm anyone.

The majority of people would find weaknesses in this argument and denounce this absurdity for what it is However, should push come to shove China could decide to support its traditional ally. This scenario is where North Korea pushes its luck, goes too far, and then bombs on the shores of Guam and makes it necessary for an attack by the U.S. to strike North Korea. China is frightened that its neighbor is being burned to death and frightened of what could occur next is the first to act and sends a huge EMP on that of the U.S. in order to block any U.S. assault in its tracks. Let's hope that the nightmare scenarios that could be envisioned will ever happen.

North Korea Makes Good on its threats

There is no way to know exactly what Kim Jong Un (or as many have called him"the "rocket man") is doing regarding his massive nuke program. There has been a lot of speculation that Kim Jong Un North Korean leader only wishes to possess a nuclear weapon to safeguard himself against any possible U.S. attempt at regime change. The argument is that even though non-nuclear states like Iraq or Libya have had to endure a gruelling regime changes, whether in a direct or indirect way, backed by and the United States, nations with nuclear weapons are safe from the encroachments of such a government.

In direct support of this notion more than any other factor is the shocking fact that the long-time leader of Libya, Momar Kaddafi actually willingly surrendered his arsenal that were used to destroy the world, which included the elements of a developing nuclear program in exchange for a promise by the Bush administration not to interfer with Libyan government. However, it took only an administration change a couple of years later to see the president Obama in charge of the effort to take Kaddafi out of his position at the time of the Arab Spring.

In the event that Kaddafi were to have a nuclear weapon to use as his Trump card, this likely wouldn't have occurred. It appears that Kim Jong Un has paid the attention to this story of a leader of the state who has embraced nuclear disarmament only to die and has taken the lessons to take to. That's why, for many, it appears that Kim is mostly bluff and braggadocio and using nuclear weapons to fend off against the United States, but would never be able to use the weapons.

There are those who would say that even if all Kim desired was a nuclear deterrent all he needed was one nuclear bomb. only one nuclear weapon is typically enough to stop an invasion of a whole country. an entire country, but Kim continued to pursue the bomb, he continued to chase two bombs and continued to go after 20 bombs. North Korea is now producing nuclear weapons, and increasingly robust and more powerful nuclear weapons at such a rapid pace that some policy analysts are now sounding alarms that a basic nuclear deterrent isn't the only issue Kim is looking for.

It appears that Kim is working on something else completely. Kim Jong Un seems to have three objectives in mind through his nuclear development to either destroy or bully South Korea and unify the whole Korean region under his rule and retaliate against Japan for the inhumane acts Japan made against the country during World War Two, and maybe drop an enormous EMP upon the United States to make it ineffective in responding (at at the very least in a timely fashion) to North Korea's assaults against its neighbors.

In this frightening hypothesis, North Korea would take away its U.S. electrical grid first with a devastating EMP followed by a bomb and/or flood troop movements to South Korea, while simultaneously destroying Japan by using nuclear conventional arms, hoping they would not be defeated. U.S. would be literally "powerless" to stop the attack. It is in a scenario such as such that U.S. needs to make sure that it's able to avoid, or largely, endure an EMP attack without damage in order it is certain that North

Korea would not be in a position to fulfill its threats.
Iran Drops Secret Bomb
Obama President Barack Obama made a deal with Iran to halt their development of nuclear technology for 10 years. However, some skeptical experts believe that Iran will likely continue to pursue its development regardless. It is also interesting that Iran already has long-rage missiles, thanks to North Korea. This fact North Korea has exported military equipment to Iran is what prompted the president George Bush to make North

Korea as well as Iran one of the countries he called the "Axis of Evil".

Surprisingly, both countries in North Korea and Iran do not share much in their common. North Korea is a communist nation that does not believe in religion. Iran is a strict religious nation. However, despite their opposing beliefs, both countries share a common tension in relation with their neighbors in the United States. This is the reason America's American CIA in the Bush administration was afraid of the two countries actively cooperating with one another.

If Iran had secretly made the bomb, or North Korea actually colluded with Iran enough to deliver the weapon already built, Iran could produce an unexpected and unpleasant shock in the form of an EMP explosion that could hit across the United States. It is a sad absurdity that the so-called axis evil could finally meet the hype and alarmists, by launching an electro magnetic version of the smoking gun.

Terrorists Set Up Suitcase EMP

In this chapter, we've discussed the risks of other countries exposing to the United States to a nationwide power outage due to the use of an EMP attack. Let's look at the uncomfortable threat of terrorists using smaller, or "Suitcase EMP" to specifically strike the power grid in the city they want to target. In this scenario, a tiny group of terrorists could eject an EMP from a suitcase in the center of the city center New York creating a city-wide blackout.

Furthermore, as the infrastructure was damaged, the terrorists are aware that it could require months to turn the power back. In the event of such an attack the blackout is likely to be the first stage of the plan. Once the power grid has been shut down, terrorists could then proceed to stage where they will expose the city to horrifying terror attacks with conventional bombings as well as mass shootings, or even stabbings.

It's a terrifying thing to contemplate and even a small suitcase could trigger terrible results. To be able to cause this damages, it's believed that the entire cost of financing such a task--which includes the gathering of all the technical components of the device -- will be less than a couple thousand dollars. This is a shocking statistic and yet another reason why experts remain up late in the never-ending struggle to ensure that the rest of us are secure.

Chapter 4: Preparing For Unexpected Blackouts

Luckily, you're not in the midst of an outage right now and there are plenty of ways to prepare your family and yourself to make it through an outage. It's always better to be prepared than to regret it. Make sure you are well-prepared and educated. Take these sensible tips while getting off the grid and live a long and prosperous life without electricity.

Alternative energy

Alternative energy is among the most beneficial things to put your hard-earned money in. It will not only assist you to survive an outage, but if it is implemented in a seamless manner, it can serve as an essential power source for the home and your home. Yes, it is an investment once but you are able to make up for it by the dramatic reduction in the cost of electricity.

Renewable energy is one of the most efficient ways to supply power to your home. There are a lot of firms that can put the Solar power station on the roof of your home. But, you are able to build a sustainable solar power plant by yourself also.

You will need a few of solar panels as well as an inverter wires, connectors, batteries and a charge control. Set it up onto your roofing and forget about your traditional source of energy. Follow these steps to make an solar panel system of your own.

1. Begin by taking your battery and join them with wires. First, connect the wires to the opposite pole, then connect them to the positive pole.

2. Attach the charger to the negative end of the battery and then connect it to the solar panel.
3. Use the same method for connecting the panels to the battery.
4. The solar panel should be placed into the sun to get charged. Set it up on the roof so that it gets enough of sunlight.
5. If the panel is charged greater than 50 percent, then you may use it to power your home equipment.

Hydropower is an alternative. If you are near an area with a stream, or have the ability to install an in-ground power plant in the backyard of your home, it is able to provide sufficient amount of power to power virtually all of the household appliances you own.

Furthermore, you may seek advantage of non-conventional sources such as biodiesel, ethanol and other sources of fuel.

Paddle Power Generator

If you don't think any of these options will work for you, there is a way to come up with an electric bicycle generator that you can build on your own. It's not just an excellent way to get work out, but you also can generate enough energy too. There are a lot of bicycle generators (also called Paddle Power Generators) that are available for purchase on the internet. If you're interested in creating your own bicycle generator on one of your own, then follow these easy steps.

1. Begin by purchasing a bicycle. It is also possible to purchase an old model at the garage sale. We would prefer an eight-speed bike, however it's not a necessity. As long as it's working, it can meet your requirements.

2. Remove the tube, as well as the tire on the back wheel, as it will be replaced with an engine.

3. Choose a drive belt and connect them to your wheels. Put the wheels so that the bike can't go forward.

4. Place the back wheel of your bicycle against one of these stands or clamps that are available for purchase.

5. Set up the arrangement in it is so that the rear wheel will be able to move freely.

6. Install the system using bolts and nuts, and then attach the back wheel to the help of a DC motor. It is also possible to use any other battery or generator here. Anything that could keep the DC current could work.

7. Be sure that all connections are made in a seamless manner. It is essential to make sure that the positive end that is the motor's anode (of the diode) and the cathode attached to the negative end of the battery.

8. Place the negative end of the motor on the negative side of the battery, too.

9. In the end, you have to connect the batteries with the converter.

10. After fixing the motor in place and connect it with the battery you must be sure that the system is functioning before taking it for a test drive. Utilize a multimeter to determine the the voltage it's generating.

In this way, you'll be able to generate sufficient amount of power to power your most essential appliances. This might not be an alternative to the standard power source or provide all your electrical requirements, but it will certainly be a big assistance during a power blackout.

Make a garden

Instead of waiting around for electricity to be restored to cook your dinner, it's always recommended to begin by planting your own garden. It is easy to eat fresh fruits and vegetables to satisfy the daily nutrient requirements of your body, without having to cook.

If you own a backyard it is possible to build a gorgeous garden in it. Be sure to keep it varied and include sections that are diverse in plants and fruits. One of the great things about owning your garden is that it allows you to easily control the kind of plants you would like to grow.

You can plant vegetables that are seasonal and enjoy various vegetables throughout the year. But, you must include some perennials too. They require little maintenance and yield a decent amount of production all through the year.

Make an effort to learn about crop rotation so that you can satisfy the requirements for your household. It will also ensure that the nutritional value of your soil stays intact. In addition, you could grow an herb garden, and grow exotic plants or spices throughout the year. Beyond just vegetables and fruits You can also grow your preferred spices inside your yard.

This may require some effort however it will result in positive outcomes over the long haul.

Raise livestock

Being off grid means that there will be no dairy or milk products. However, you could live without them, but you're not sure of the length of time a blackout could last. In the worst-case scenario, it is possible that you may be forced to endure months (or perhaps even for months) without power. It is crucial that you plan for the worst case scenario and emerge as the one who survived.

Begin by raising goats cows, or sheep for milk production. You can purchase a few youngsters from an animal farm and set up an appropriate space within your yard. If you have the space and space, you must think about constructing an coop for chickens. In addition to being utilized for meat production as well, but they also produce eggs, too.

Cubby holes can be created inside your chicken coop in order to get eggs and also have an appropriate space too. In the event of a crisis you are able to offer or exchange your animal to get by.

Food preservation

In the absence of electricity, you may not be able to use a refrigerator that is functional and you may not be able preserve food items. However, you must have plenty of canned foods, however not every food item is able to be canned. If you've got vegetables, fruits meat, eggs, or milk, it is likely that you'll need an option to keep these items.

You could either design an mini-refrigerator on your own or can these items also. We recommend purchasing an automatic pressure canner. It will make the process of canning much simpler. It will be possible to can slices of fruit, meat and other veggies without trouble. This will allow you to prolong the life of these products significantly.

You can also contemplate picking the foods you eat. However it is true that not all food items could be transformed into pickles, however you can make pickles of your favourite vegetables and fruits with ease. It is an ideal substitute for food in winter months when you don't have accessibility to fresh food items. Choose to eat dry fruits and vegetables in the event that you are unable to keep them refrigerated. Dry fruits are not just tasty, they also have lots of nutrients too. They also do not require electricity to preserve them.

There are refrigerators that are able to run for as long as 10 days without power. You can buy one of these products or make your own. Sand is among the most suitable materials for creating the fridge-in-a-pot. You can make a tiny pot refrigerator by following these steps.

1. Make sure you have two large sand buckets each one smaller than the one. Make sure the smaller one can be capable of fitting inside that larger pot.
2. Create holes in the bottom of both pots and then use the clay or paste to fill them.
3. The bottom of the larger one with sand. Place the smaller pot inside it.
4. Sand the entire pot, and fill in the gaps, while leaving the opening of the pot unbroken.
5. Soak the sand in cold water.
6. Cover it with clothing and fabric, and let it cool off.
7. Put it in a well-ventilated area and store your fruits and veggies inside to ensure they are fresh.

These simple methods will help you brainstorm various ways to live without power. Make sure to implement these ideas one at a time and ensure you're prepared for any unexpected power loss.

Chapter 5: Home Preparation

It is not enough to prepare intended for EMP attacks, but also for all other catastrophes too that means you're going be required to begin by identifying the kinds of catastrophes most likely to impact your area. On a piece of paper that is on the left on the page, note all possible disasters that could be a threat to your area beginning with EMP. Make an area in the middle of the page and write down any items that are be likely to cause disruption, i.e. electricity and water. In the left area of your paper note down what you'll need to take care of when the disasters you've identified happen. It is possible to consider making a 72-hour emergency kit, or a 3-4 week kit or even a kit suitable for longer than two months. The strategy focuses on the way to solve the catastrophe, not on the cause of the disaster.

Self-reliance is a different topic. It is crucial to be equipped with the fundamentals of self-reliance. This will help people be prepared for challenges that may occur due to an EMP or natural disaster. Self-reliance is a way to prepare prior to a natural disaster strikes them. It is crucial to have an emergency food supply for three months that can be a included in the family's regular food plan. As time passes the family will be able to build more food storage space that can last for one year. It is essential to build gradually a long-term food storage as drinking water comes at the top in the list. Storing water won't just help a family, but also keeps the family safe from getting sick from water that has been polluted. Beans, wheat and rice can last for as long as 30 years. These are essential staples for families to buy as soon as you begin to grow you food store.

When it comes to the storage of water over the long haul the first thing you're going to have to ensure is that you pick the correct container to store the water. If you do not take this step and just use whatever is available, you risk thinking that you're prepared but then finding out that in the worst moment, that all the water you drink is affected. Although not all plastics can be used for long-term storage of water, plastics with the number of 1, 4, and 5 can all be utilized to store water for long periods of time. If, however, you are seeking the most effective storage solution for water, then you'll need to consider a stainless-steel water container. Not only are they popular, meaning they can be purchased at a bargain price however the water contained inside them can be stored for as long as 40 years.

Another major issue with water storage is the location. The right place to store your water is crucial to ensure the water you use is potable over the long run. That means that you're going to have to pick an area that is solid and safe from the immediate direction of any disasters that you'd like to avoid. Also, it should be in a location that is dark cool, and dry. Additionally, it is essential to ensure that you don't rupture the seal of your water until the time you intend to drink it. Even though the water you drink could be usable for as long as 40 years, it's recommended to change it every six months if you are able to do this. By doing this, you can make sure that the water remains in top shape that you can get it in when you need it.

It is also crucial to think about how you will plan cleaning the water you store after you've exhausted your reserve and your overall situation isn't improving. The first element you are always required to add will be chlorine. In particular, you're likely to need to add two drops and just 2 drops for every two Liters of water being stored. After you have added the chlorine, you'll be required to keep the bottle open for at minimum an hour before drinking.

To accommodate the demands for larger quantities of water, you're likely to require poolshock on hand. The official title for the product is calcium hypochlorite. A single pound will purify 10,000 gallons. When buying it, it is essential that you choose a an item that is between an 80% and 78 percent purity. It must also be free of any softeners for water. If you're prepared in this manner you'll be provided with water.

If disaster strikes the good news is that yourself and the rest of your household will not suffer from thirst.

The home preparation process is not just about items that can be used to prepare for a catastrophe. It is equally important to be aware of the event. This includes knowing what to do prior to, during, and following the catastrophe. Education is the key to surviving. We also need to teach others to be able to survive if the worst happens.

Another thing to consider is to ensure that the family and you members are well-nourished and physically fit. Get exposed to a diverse selection of meals and ensure that you are already enjoying an array of canned choices to make the transition as smooth as possible. Avoid alcohol, caffeine as well as harmful drugs. This is not only good suggestion in general however, it also means that you don't need to worry about the withdrawal symptoms as well as the other things that are taking place after a natural disaster is ravaging your home and you need to fight for survival.

The process of saving money is also a an aspect of the process. If you're employed, be sure to save a portion of your earnings. This is not only to invest however, also to cover emergency needs. Even if the force of the catastrophe is such that it seems that, at the very least that things will never return the way they were, it will be some time when having cash on hand can be an excellent bartering tool. If things don't look too bad in the near future, cash will come to become more essential because there isn't the infrastructure that can support other kinds of transactions. Given the amount of cash that is carried around, just a few thousand dollars in your account is likely to be enough to make you feel like the kings of the world until infrastructure can be restored.

Work with people in the community. Follow the guidelines the government might have. Help those in need if in a position to. When the community works together, the process will be much easier.

Chapter 6: Basic Urban Survival Skills

In a urban setting, surviving after a catastrophe of this magnitude like an EMP attack is going to require you to master several important, specific capabilities.

Here are the most basic urban survival skills you'll require to master:

Situational Awareness

The very first skill you'll have to master is the ability to be aware of your surroundings. Situational awareness simply means how well-aware you are of the surroundings around you. You pay attention to things like the conversations that are going on in the surrounding area, exit points as you enter the building for the first time, searching for anything that aren't normal as well as who is entering and leaving the building.

It is essentially, that you will learn how to pay attention to your surroundings and live in the present, rather than snoozing or daydreaming.

Self-Defense and Security

Another important aspect to be taught is self-defense. The rate of crime will increase following a major catastrophe that strikes urban areas. There will be massive crowds, organized raiding parties as well as looters and individuals who break into homes.

The ability to recognize situations is the first step in learning self-defense. The second is the capability to protect yourself. You must have tools which allow you to defend yourself including knives and Tasers, pepper spray or any other firearms that can be carried around your body.

First Aid

Following a catastrophic event there is a chance that you won't be able to access doctors or medical professionals. You'll need a comprehensive first aid kit, including one at home, and another in your car. Additionally, you'll need to master basic first aid techniques including setting a limp that has been dislocated or stopping the bleeding from an open wound and then treating it, as well as treating the broken limb or splint.

The process of becoming a gray Man (or woman)

Gray men (or woman) is someone who blends into their surroundings, and stay away from being recognized.

Strategies to become gray men include:

- Dress in the same type of clothes the people around you are wearing.
- Always follow the current of a crowd and not against it.

Avoid wearing backpacks, if at all possible.

Do not look at anyone

Never make a challenge to anyone

Keep your head at a low level

Store any valuable items or weapons hidden

Finding Your Way Home

The search for your way back home is the top priority after a major catastrophe strikes your city. You might think you'll return home by car but it won't be that easy. One thing is that the roads will be congested and, as a consequence from the effects of an EMP Attack or Solar Flare The majority of vehicles won't work!

So, it is essential to be able to have primary, secondary and tertiary routes in place to return home on the foot. The routes should be avoided in areas that are particularly crowded, and risky including intersections and major stores (as they are likely to be taken away) bridges, tunnels, bridges and government buildings.

It is also necessary to have a bag for getting home or a small bag of emergency items are easy to carry to assist you in getting back home.

At a minimum, this take home bag must include the following items:

Tactical Folding Knife

Pay in cash ($100 minimum, split in bills smaller)

- Bottle of water Bottle

Personal Water Filter

- Fire Starter

Flashlight

- Protein Bar

The Basic First Aid Kit

Map and Compass Map and Compass

The only downside to carrying a bag to get home is that carrying a backpack will make you a target for your back because it is noticeable in the crowd. People who are desperate are likely to identify a backpack as having important items, so make sure to select smaller bags that will be more concealable and also be sure to keep secure to your.

Scavenging

The next important urban survival technique you'll require is the ability to find materials in an urban setting.

In particular, you'll be required to learn how to find food water, food, emergency equipment, and essential survival equipment.

When it comes to which are the best locations to get your hands on a scavenge your best bets would be one or all of these:

-- Grocery stores and shopping malls (will be taken, but worth taking a look)
- Churches
- Sporting Goods Stores
Restaurants
- Manufacturing Facilities/Warehouses
- Marinas/Shipping Yards

Schools

Construction Sites Construction Sites

Hospitals

Bartering

Last but not least, the most important ability you'll need to master is negotiation and bartering. After a catastrophe the only way to increase your resources is through scavenging or bartering.

Make sure you have things that you are able to barter with to exchange (this is the reason why it's so important to build a second inventory of things to barter with as well as the main stockpile).

Always take at least 2 other people in the event of bartering. Be prepared, and be with binoculars, or a rifle scope far away. You must also be able to walk away and never demonstrate that you're desperate or make your first bargaining offer.

Security Options

Security should be a top priority in any disaster that strikes the city. How can you invest your time and money to put together an emergency supply, only to then have it be taken by a robber or a raiding group.

The lives of your family members will be extremely vulnerable if you do not set at least a few security measures for your home.

The typical American house is extremely vulnerable to burglaries and attacks that's the reason you'll need to alter the layout of your property and home in order to make it less difficult to get into.

In that light Here are some fundamental security choices to think about:

Heavy Duty Fortified Doors

Most doors are constructed of wood, and they can be easily broken down using either sledgehammers or an axe and the locks and bolts aren't as strong. You can fix this issue by replacing all doors that open to the out to the outside using metal doors and replacing the bolts and locks with heavy strong versions.

Acrylic Glass Windows

In addition to your doors, windows are the second most evident entryway. Glass is easily broken down, and so you'll need to replace your glass windows by using acrylic glass that looks exactly the same, but is much more durable.

Warning Signals

Signs of caution like "beware of guard dogs" and "trespassers will be killed" could help in making potential burglars take a second look.

Security Cameras

Security cameras offer an advantage of keeping watch on the exterior of your house and the surrounding area. It's important to remember that if power is down all over the place, the security cameras won't operate as effectively. However, the security cameras set up around your house could provide the same results as warning signs , in that they could help discourage potential intruders.

Tripwire

The most basic home security solution is to create a tripwire along the outside of your home. Be sure to set it at a low level to ensure it's not easy to spot.

Perimeter Alarm

Extend the tripwire concept by attaching tins packed with pebbles to your tripwire. they'll vibrate whenever they're disturbed, alerting your to intruders. U.S. Marines used this technique to great effect during the Pacific Theater of World War II.

Turn Your Landscape Into A Natural Defense

If you plant thorny thickets or brush, like blackberry or rose bushes, you could aid in preventing group of potential attackers or at the very least slow their movement. You can cover your entire property with thorny brush If you wish to, or you can plant them in the weakest points for example, near your windows.

Create Your House Look Clean

By using this method, you can make your home appear like it's as run-down as you could. You can smash down windows and doors, paint on the exterior take down the lawn, scatter trash all over It's all you need to do. This is definitely an opportunity to gamble because it's not guaranteed that raiding groups will continue (believing your home has been abandoned and they might attempt to steal from it). However, it's a good idea.

Dogs

Dogs are also a huge threat to burglars. If you have larger security dogs, you are able to really put fear into the hearts of burglars and groups of thieves. Even a tiny dog can be more effective than nothing, since they could identify burglars, too.

Pit Trap

Much like we've seen in TV and movies shows it is possible to dig a hole, put spikes in the bottom before covering the entire top of it in tarp or a plant. Anyone who falls into it will not be very content at all, let's say.

Barbed Wire Fence

Install a barbed wire fence around the boundary of your property to create a protection for anyone who wants to cross. You can put barbed wire in the middle of the fence you have already put up or even install stakes into the ground and connect barbed wire to them.

Nail Boards

Choose a flat piece of plywood, put some nails in it. then turn upside down and then set it lying on the floor. You can cover them up or leave them open to deter the intruders.

Insuring Your House

These are merely a few basics security tips on ways to increase your home's security and your property. It's unlikely that you'll be able to implement all of them, but applying just two or three will go a long way in making your home or property safer following a grid collapse.

Security for Your Home

Let's go over a simple step-by step method to put up defensive fortifications, and put up an effective defense for your home in the event of a natural disaster:

Step #1 - Make an investment in defensive Weaponry

First of all, you must have arms of defense that you can actually, defend yourself with!

Particularly, you'll need firearms. We live in a time of guns. Tasers and pepper spray are fantastic personal defense weapons, but they're enough when it comes to mounting an effective defense for your house.

Three specific weapons you'll need to protect your home include:
- Handgun (9mm, .40 S&W, .45 ACP, .38 Special, .357 Magnum)
- - Shotgun (12 Gauge, or 20 gauge)
Semi-Automatic Rifle (5.56x45mm NATO or 7.62x39mm)

Of the three firearms, the handgun will be the most crucial one, for the simple reason that it is able to be hidden on your person and will provide an enormous benefit. The shotgun is the second most crucial, after that, the rifle is third. Make sure you have at the least 1,000 rounds for each firearm (that might sound like a lot however, it's not).

Step #2 - Secure your doors and Windows
They are the apparent entryways, therefore they must be strengthened first. Replace all wood doors that lead out to the exterior with doors made of steel and change all locks with stronger models. Windows need to be replaced by stronger

acrylic glass or alternatively, be strengthened by chickenwire.

Step #3 - Construct A Defensive Perimeter

Your home's security is always more effective if you stop the attackers from entering of your property, and the most effective method to accomplish this is to build an effective perimeter.

The most efficient and easy security measure is to create a barbed-wire fence around your property. You can connect barbed wire to the fence you have already put up or put stakes into the ground , and then run barbed wire through them.

If you want to go an extra mile, create a second barbed-wire fence to the left of the first and you could also install a layer of nail boards between these two. Anyone who would attempt to launch an offensive from front against that type of defensive fortification would be a fool.

Step 4: Invest In Sandbags

Sandbags are the most effective method of absorbing ammunition should your home come under attack. You should set the sandbags in strategic locations for example, the windows and doors behind you.

To store sandbagsin storage, it is best to keep the bags and sand in separate containers and then add the sand to bags once it is time to construct the protection of your home.

Step 5 - Set Up An Alert System

In the next step, you'll need create an alarm system that will make you aware of any intrusion. The most effective method to do this is to make an area of trip wire and then place the tin cans stuffed with pebbles in regular intervals in the wire. When the tripwire gets disrupted, the pebbles vibrate.

Step #6 - Warn Signs

If someone is considering taking over your property the chance to see that you're serious about business. If the fortifications above did not already scream you could put up signs that are spelled out to read "trespassers are going to be killed!"

To enhance the effect, make shotguns and rifles visible from windows. Make the warnings visible, so that they are easily read. I hope that anyone who thinks of an attack , they will reconsider the plan and then move to a different house.

Step 7 - Work with Your Neighbors

You should work with your neighbors, rather than fighting them. It's likely that your neighbors won't be prepared at all. They'll be without food, things similar to that, which means they are likely to become desperate if the catastrophe lasts for a long time.

The likelihood of your neighbors turning against the situation is very real, however, you can turn the situation around by convening a meeting of your neighbors after the tragedy has occurred to work together to come up with an plan of action. The idea of setting up a watch for your neighborhood by assigning roles your neighbors is a great way to strengthen your protection against attacks from outside.

Step #8 – Be Prepared

Be vigilant in case catastrophe strikes. After the stores have been gone, the mobs as well as the robbers will take over suburban homes later.

In general, don't let a family member leave the home unless there is a legitimate reason (such as the run to scavenge or get together with someone other). Always keep a firearm or revolver on your hip always, so that you are able to access a firearm immediately in the situation in the event of an emergency.

Alternative Light Sources and Heat Sources
Today , in America, in the United States, all homes are heated due to an international building code that is used to ensure that every home remains within a certain "comfort zone.'

The issue is that people become used to the idea of having heating. Also they have it as a given. If the grid of electricity were to fail (and someday it could happen) What other heat and light sources would you look to in the event of a power outage?

What do you think? Almost all homes with heating depend on electricity. If the grid is cut then the power.

Here are the top alternative sources of light and heat you can use:

1 - Candles

The first choice is candles. Every kit for emergency at home has to have candles on hand to go. Candles are simple to light and to use, and have no expiration dates.

The only issue with them is that they're a bit risky. If you knock one over, it could ignite the fire. This is a serious risk when you have kids running around.

However, they do give you an instant source of warmth and light. There are also candles that last for over fifty hours before you leave.

2. Catalytic Heater

Catalytic heaters are highly efficient and efficiently burns. They rely on an element of ceramic with a bed that burns gas to bring warmth to the area. You can purchase catalytic heaters with a range of sizes, certain models are designed to fit small spaces and others for larger rooms. Catalytic heaters are not dependent on electricity and are typically priced between $200 and $300.

3. Flashlight

A bit obvious, yes however, it is still worthwhile to mention. It is recommended to have several flashlights of different types that you have in your arsenal as well as a huge supply of batteries. They don't usually provide warmth, but they almost certainly give you lighting.

4 - Kerosene Heater

One of the most effective alternatives to a different heater is a kerosene heating system as they are the cleanest burning heaters on the market and provide plenty of warmth.

One of the greatest benefits of a kerosene heater is that it radiates warmth from all directions and will allow you to get the maximum amount of heat you can.

The only drawback is that you must keep plenty of kerosene in stock to be able to count on it for a primary wood-burning alternative. Also in the event that you are unable to get Kerosene, you'll run out of energy (unless there are other alternatives for heat and you absolutely should).

5 - Propane Lamp

It is likely that you have heard of propane lamps on camping trips. Although they're an excellent alternative to keep in your bag but you must be cautious before using as your primary heating source.

One thing to note is that you should only use propane lamps outside or in a very well ventilated location due to them being able to pump out lots of oxygen and lots of heat. They might not be the best option for your home due to this reason.

In addition, you're dependent on the amount of propane tanks you've got available in case you decide to use an propane torch.

6 . Wood Burning Stove

And lastly, we will talk about the wood-burning stove! It's probably the oldest method of provide a room with warmth. You'll need the stove or chimney pipe, a piece of wood to burn and fireplace-starting device.

A chimney is an important feature which you can't ignore when you have the wood-burning stove. Smoke will be produced by burning the flame and needs an escape route and escape, which is why it's not the case that you just need to buy the stove, put it in any space in your home, and begin the process of burning wood within it (well you could however, that would not be very secure). There must be a chimney and that's it.

Chapter 7: Food And Water

Drinking water and food is vital. Without them, or a way for making them safe to consume or drink and drink, you'll starve to death or die of dehydration. It's that easy.

Thus, water and food must be at the first place on your list of priorities.

Here's a list the items for water and food you should keep in your refrigerator.

Coleman 5 Gallon Water Carrier

A way to store and move water is essential. I suggest using the Coleman five gallon water container. A water tank that is fully filled can provide the family of five sufficient drinking and sanitation water to last for a day (remember the 1-1-1 Rule: One gallon for each person, per day).

The water carrier can be able to fold down flatly for storage or transportation for storage and transportation purposes. It is constructed with a sturdy polyethylene material. It's FDA certified as well.

A LifeStraw personal water filter for you.

Many people around the world utilize this water filter that can be carried around in your waist or tied in your collar. You can drink straight from any source of water provided that the water isn't contaminated with chemicals. It will eliminate 99.999999 percent of parasites as well as bacteria.

It is also able to filter up to a thousand milliliters of water before it has to be replaced. It is in compliance with all EPA standards. The total length is 9 inches, and weight is 2 1 ounces.

A LifeStraw family water purifier for the entire Family.

If you are looking for a water filter for your family I suggest the LifeStraw family water purifier. It is capable of purifying 5 thousand Gallons of water before it needs to be replaced. Additionally, it's easy to use: just pour water over the top and the water that is clean is then drained into the base. The flow rate total will be 12 hours every hour.

Water

Be sure to keep the water that is clean! Place it in those 5-gallon Coleman containers that I mentioned earlier as well as in large 55 gallon drums, too.

Rememberthat you require one gallon of drinking water for each person every day, so you must make calculations based upon how long you'll need to store the water for and the number of people within your family.

As a general guideline, turn your water once per year (though at least once every six months is more secure).

Never store your water outdoors or in the sun.

For the remainder of this chapter, we'll provide a bullet-point list of foods you must store and a brief description of each of them:

* Sugar (store for a long time if it is you are air tight; Do not add any oxygen absorber)
* Salt (great for flavoringand flavoring) it is loaded with electrolytes; it can store up to 4 pounds per person each year)
* Honey (lasts for a long time, and is an excellent anti-biotic for colds, sore throats, and sore throats.)

*White Rice (white rice only Do not keep brown rice in the refrigerator for storage; shelf time is 10 years.)

* Beans (pretty anything) beans can be used for storageand are an excellent meat substitute shelf time is 10 years)

* Oats (will last for 30 years, and you only require hot water to drink and you can also utilize it for animal feed)

* Flour (great to make bread with simply mix it with water)

* Pasta (pasta can last up to 2 years if it's airtight)

* Milk Powdered (store 16 lbs per year, per person.)

* Cheese Powdered (when airtight is sealed, it has a shelf life for 10 years)

In addition to the foods, I recommend you to store Victory Gardens heirloom seeds for your garden and also an oven that has temperatures of between two hundred to two hundred fifty F.

A Global Sun Oven or All American Sun Oven is an excellent option for sun ovens.

Powerless Tools

Because the EMP attack is guaranteed to destroy all power sources You'll need to reserve powerless tools which, well, don't require power!

Below is the list with powerless tools that you can store:

Shovel

A simple shovel is sufficient and I wouldn't suggest particular brand over the other. Shovels are ideal to dig holes for building shelters as well as gardening. They can be employed as a weapon of defense when needed (such such as M48's Tactical Shovel).

Nexis Gas Shut Off Pipe Wrench

If you're dealing with any problems with your sewage system Pipe wrenches will be your ideal tool. Of course, let's make sure you don't have plumbing issues at all.

General Purpose Tools You Should Be Having On Hand

Here's a list of general-purpose tools that you'll need in your arsenal:

- Screwdriver

Hammer Hammer

- Battery Tester

Air Pump (for an bicycle)
- - Cross Cut Saw
Hacksaw Hacksaw
- Steel Pipe
Hand Drill
KA-BAR Fixed Blade Fighting Knife

Fixed blade knives are essential. The possibilities for a knife are endless and possibly even endless.

This KA-BAR model is my first option for fixed blade knives. It is made from 1095 steel, with seven inches of blade and comes with a wood or synthetic hand.

The KA-BAR has been utilized by military units throughout the world. It is the most sought-after design of fixed blade combat knife that has ever been made. It comes with a genuine sheath made of leather as well.

Buck Knives Redpoint Tactical Folding Knife

Apart from having a fixed blade knife I strongly suggest that you own a folding knife and carry around in your belt or inside your pocket.

I carry my Buck Knives Redpoint in my EDC and have discovered it extremely comfortable and sharp knife.
Here's a list characteristics it includes:

2 and 3/4 inches blade
-- Serrated Blade
428 HC Stainless Steel Blade (titanium coated)
- Non-Reflective Coating
- 2.9 Ounces
4 Inches Long (when closed)
Rubber Molded Grip (yellow or black)
Breaker Glass Breaker
- Seatbelt Cutter
Husqvarna Wooden Multi-Purpose Axe
Actually, any good axe can be used, but I'll suggest the Multi-Purpose axe by Husqvarna. The handle is made of hickory. The blade is secured by the leather sheath..
The axe is useful to smash down anything from the door lock to cutting wood.
Weapons

One thing you'll need to be ready to deal in the aftermath of an EMP attack is looters as well as raiders.

People who are desperate will do anything to stay alive which means they'll be prepared to kill your family members and yourself when they are able to believe that you're stocked with food or other things that are essential.

So, you should have an the arsenal of firearms the ability to defend your property and home at all times.

In addition to the guns be sure to stockpile at least 1o00 rounds per caliber, stored in green army boxes made of metal.

Although guns can be expensive and you might think that having a "complete arsenal of firearms' is way from your budget.

What would you say if I told you it is possible to build an entire arsenal of survival firearms for less than $2,000?

There are five distinct kinds of guns that I believe you must include within your collection.

These guns are:

-- .22 Semi-Automatic Rifle
- 12 Gauge Pump Action Shotgun
9mm Semi-Automatic Pistol
-- 5.56x45mm Semi-Automatic Rifle
- .308 Bolt Action Rifle

You can get high-quality and reliable makes and models for these guns for just two thousand dollars (give or take one hundred or even two).

Here are my suggestions of low-cost, but high-quality makes or models that you must keep in your arsenal for survival:

.22 Semi-Automatic Rifle Ruger 10-22 ($200)

It is a .22 firearm is very multi-faceted firearm. The following are the benefits of having one:

General Plinking/Casual Shoting
Pest Control - Pest Control
-- Small Game Hunting
Self-Defense (not the best option but it is a possibility to be employed)
Low Noise
- Nearly Non-Existent Recoil
- Ammo is small and can be stored in Bulk

It is one of the most well-known .22 rifle ever produced and is among the most sought-after and customizable firearms in the world. Since the 1960s, it is extremely tough and stable.

Ruger 10-22 guns are frequently available for sale at around $200 with a price range of 50 dollars or more. They are supplied with standard 10 round magazines. However, larger 25, round magazine are often also available.

12 Gauge Pump Action Shotgun: Maverick 88 ($200)

The most versatile weapon available in addition to that of .22 weapon is the shotgun with a 12 gauge. Here's why:

Use birdshot loads for small game and bird hunting

- Use buckshot loads for home defense

Use slugs to go on the big game (within greater distances)

The Maverick pump action shotgun is the cheapest variant that is a cheaper version of the Mossberg 500 which is among the most sought-after shotguns ever made. The shotgun 590A1 from Mossberg is the sole pump gun that has been able to be able to pass an examination by the U.S Army's torturing test.

Maverick 88 Maverick 88 does not come with the features of those of the Mossberg 500, but it is equipped with the same standard of reliability and quality.

I'd suggest you purchase a combination Maverick 88 which has the shortest 18.5 inch gun barrel that is ideal for defense at home, and the longer 26-inch and 28-inch vented rib to hunt with.

9mm Semi-Automatic Pistol Glock 19. ($500)

The next step will be the pistol 9mm that can be used for the following reasons:

Concealed Carry

Backup Weapon for Rifle

General For All Purposes Sidearm

Home Defense Home Defense

It is without doubt that without a doubt, the Glock 19 is the 9mm pistol I would recommend to use as your EMP sidearm to attack. The Glock pistol has been proven to be extremely durable and well-known. Accessories and spare parts are plentiful. It is the Glock 19 in particular is their most popular model. Field stripping and maintenance is incredibly simple.

However, the reason I would recommend G19 over other models of Glock is that the G19 above other Glock models from Glock is that it's small and simple to conceal, yet it can hold the ammunition of 15 rounds and one inside the chamber.

The G19 can also take Glock 17 17-round magazines, or extra 33 round magazines, too.

Of course, there are other semi-automatic pistols that are reliable at the same price too. The Walther P99/PPQ Beretta the 92FS Beretta PX4, Smith & Wesson M&P along with the Springfield XD come to mind.

All of them are excellent guns too, but it is the Glock 19 is still more well-known than any of them therefore spare magazines and other parts are much easier to find.

5.56x45mm Semi-Automatic Rifle: Smith &Wesson M&P15 Sport II ($500)

Your 5.56x45mm semi-automatic rifle can be used to safeguard your home and your family from multiple threats. It has more capability and range over the pistol or shotgun and lower recoil than a shotgun , and more stopping force than the pistol.

It is also possible to utilize this rifle to hunt smaller game species, like hunting wild boars, deer or pronghorn. But, it's too heavy for larger game like elk or moose.

The AR-15 is, without doubt, the most reliable semi-automatic rifle to perform this purpose. It's the most sought-after centerfire weapon sold in America. Accessories and spare parts are readily available through.

If you are looking for a low-cost AR-15 from a reputable manufacturer, I suggest that you purchase the S&W M&P15 Sport II. It is recommended to select this Sport II model because the Sport I lacks a forward assist and dust cover which can improve the reliability of the gun in difficult conditions.

If you want to replace the S&W alternative, you can opt for the Ruger AR-556 that is similar with that of the M&P with regards to cost and quality.

.308 Bolt Action Rifle: Mossberg Patriot ($400)

Then, last but not least it's time to talk about this rifle, the .308 bolt-action rifle. This is the type of rifle can be used for large game hunting. It could also be used to protect yourself from armed threats at large distances, too.

If you are looking for a low-cost but of high-end .308 firearm, I suggest that you consider the Mossberg Patriot. In particular, consider the model that includes an Vortex scope that is already mounted on the rifle.

I frequently find I often see the Mossberg Patriot + Scope combo priced at $400 or lower than that at times. It is possible that the low price implies that the Patriot isn't expensively constructed however, it actually is equipped with a high-quality wooden or synthetic stock and shoots in tight groups.

Mossberg is a name that is well-known for their top-quality products, as well (the Mossberg 500 is my preferred choice for shooting guns).

When you add these figures together we'll be spending around $1,800 for the five weapons. Add sales tax, and you'll end up spending close to $2,000, yet we're in the budget.

Naturally, you'll have to purchase more ammunition and spare magazines and slings, holsters, and more. In the end, you'll be spending more than $2,000.

However, you're not paying money to acquire an entire arsenal of high-quality guns.

If $2,000 still seems like a lot of money Don't be tempted to purchase every gun in one go. You can purchase only one if would prefer to do so.

Chapter 8: The Most Important Types Of Guns To Include In Your Armory

The creation of an armory for your personal is among the most crucial things is possible to do as a preparedness expert. It's on par with water, food and medicines. The reason behind this is that security has to be the primary concern for you. It is essential to be prepared to protect yourself in the event of an SHTF situation simply. If you don't have a plan, there's no way you'll be able to survive if others have plans to kill your family and steal everything you've got.

So regardless of whether or not you have guns at present or not, it is a good idea to must to start creating your own personal armoury. There are no guns that can be used to build your armory.

Instead, there are certain areas that you must cover to ensure that your arsenal is as complete and flexible as it can be.

Here are the top types of firearms you could own:

A .22 Rifle

The first gun you will have to have in the arsenal of yours is the most common ever the .22 LR, and hopefully an automatic semi-automatic that is reliable.

An .22 rifle is among the most useful weapons to keep in your arsenal. From target shooting , plinking to pest control , to teaching novice shooters to hunting small game and the fact that ammunition is cheap and plentiful, to the purpose of defense (yes it is true that a .22 can be used in self-defense even though it is small caliber) The benefits of having the .22 can be infinite.

A gun collection is not complete without an .22 rifle in addition, the .22 LR itself is very often overlooked by people.

There are a variety of types of .22 semi-automatic rifles you might choose and 3 of the more well-known options are Ruger's 10/22, the Marlin Model 60, and the Smith and Wesson M&P15-22.

A Shotgun

Another option is a shotgun. It could be even more important to own than an .22

or .22, but certainly to be used in self-defense.

A shotgun is great because it allows you to feed it three different types of ammunition that can serve three different functions.

The different types of ammunition and uses are:

1. Birdshot: To capture birds or Small Game Hunting
2. Buckshot: the Home Defense and Combat
3. Slugs: Ideal for Big Game Hunting (within moderate distances)

In reality, if you look at it this way the only two things that a shotgun can't be used for are long-range shooting and concealed carry (at least , not in the practical sense for the former).

Choose a 12 gauge pump action model too. It is the most well-known shotgun caliber, which means it will be the most common. It is possible to consider 20 gauge if are looking for a shotgun with less recoil, however 12 gauge is more popular.

It is advisable to opt for pumps as well since pump action shotguns are less expensive and more durable than semi-autos. The most expensive semi-automatic shotguns are reliable sure, but the pump action is purchased for a fraction of the cost.

If you are looking for a pump action shotgun with 12 gauge and a 12 gauge shotgun, the Remington 870 and Mossberg 500 are two of the best choices. Both are great and are available at less than $500.

A Handgun

An argument that is convincing and persuasive could be made to the effect that firearms for hand are the most essential weapon to own due to the simple reason that it is able to be concealed and in a concealed manner within your body. This is an important benefit that you won't draw unwanted attention to you.

Additionally, a handgun may be carried with you in all times, which means you'll be able to pull it out quickly in an emergency situation if you need to, while the shotgun or rifle may be kept a distance from you.

For a handgun choose a semi-automatic 9mm. 9mm is the most abundant and inexpensive pistol round and is suitable for self-defense , when loaded with the appropriate ammunition. Semi-automatic 9mm pistols also have large capacity magazines of 15-20 rounds, depending on the firearm and the magazine, making them an excellent option to defend against numerous attackers.

Some 9mm handguns can be used as your SHTF weapon could include: Beretta 92, Beretta Px4, Canik TP9, Glock 17, SIG P226/P229 SIG P320 Smith & Wesson M&P, Springfield XD, Taurus PT92 and that of the Walther PPQ.

A Rifle for Defense

The next step is to get an assault rifle that is semi-automatic and an intermediate cartridge, such as 5.56x45mm NATO.

The defensive semi-auto rifle provides more range than the shotgun or pistol. It can also be fired from long distances and is the most reliable weapon to work to defend against several adversaries.

If you want to have a rifle for defense it's a no-brainer to opt for an AR-15. It's the rifle of America and the modern-day musket is among the most widely used and customisable firearms that are available. There are three models: the Del-Ton DT-15, Ruger AR-556, and Smith &Wesson M&P15 Sports II are all high quality ARs you can purchase for about $500, perhaps even.

A Hunting Rifle

Not least, you'll need a hunting gun with a scope as well as an increased caliber that can be used to take down large game , or even attackers over large distances.

There's an array of calibers you can choose to hunt with However .308 or .30-06 are the most popular.

If money is a problem There are plenty of hunting rifles with budget prices available as combos that include scopes that are available for purchase at under $400. Ruger American and Mossberg Patriot are two of them. Ruger American and

Mossberg Patriot are two of the best examples.

The Top Survivability Rifles to have in Your Arsenal

What are the best survival rifles you could include in your collection? you might ask?

To to answer this question We'll review some of the most popular brands and types of guns that you can take into consideration.

There's no need to own each rifle we're about to discuss. The point of this list is simply to provide some thoughts about the various types of rifles readily available.

Sorted alphabetically In alphabetical order, here are the following:

AK-47

In terms of the specific brands, Arsenal probably makes the most effective AK-47s available in the present. For instance, the Century Arms C39V2 and RAS-47 along with the WASR-10 are all high-quality AK-47s which can be purchased for less money.

The AK-47 is a semi-automatic rifle that chambers to take 7.62x39mm round.

7.62x39mm round. This has some power over that of the 5.56x45mm NATO. The AK-47 is well-known for its durability and durability, but its it isn't the most accurate offered by other rifles.

AR-15

The most popular of AR-15 rifles is Colt LE6920 however, they are also available at an expensive price. There is also the Ruger AR-556 and the Smith &Wesson M&P15 Sport II are two other AR-15s designed to last which are available at a fraction of the price.

The AR-15 is by far the top centerfire rifle that is currently in high demand. It's comfortable, it's adjustable, the accessories are plentiful and it's very easy to master the art of shooting. As a survival rifle it is a great weapon to defend yourself and hunting large deer game.

Marlin 336

Lever action .30-30 rifle comes with many advantages. It's extremely compact and compactly packed into cars It's not as intimidating as a semi-automaticgun, and it provides an increased rate of fire than a bolt-action.

The 336 Marlin is a prime example of a top lever action carbine that is .30-30 that you can purchase at under $400. The primary selling point of 336 over Winchester 1894 is that the spent shell casings release from the side instead of via the upper part, which allows the user to attach the scope or red dot if you wish.

Marlin 1895

If you are looking for a rifle with a lever action that has more force that the .30-30 round and this Marlin 1895 .45-70 is an excellent choice to consider. It has plenty of power however it is not able to shoot anything that is in North America.

Ruger 10/22

It is important not to undervalue it .22 LR for survival purposes. It is a great round to use efficiently to hunt small game, to defend (if needed) as a plinking weapon as well as for pest control as well as to teach people about shooting. It's also a cheap round that is available in large quantities, requires little room for storage, and it's quiet and has a very low recoil.

The Ruger 10/22 rifle is among the most sought-after .22 rifle available. It's also a highly adjustable gun, much like the AR-15. Ruger also offers an Takedown model which you can easily split into two parts to store.

Ruger Gunsite Scout Rifle (GSR)

Ruger Gunsite Scout Rifle, or GSR represents the highest point of the Scout rifle idea as it was conceived by Jeff Cooper, who wanted an .308 bolt-action carbine that had an detachable magazine as well as an optic in front to the front of the receiver.

Cooper claimed that the Scout rifle is the only rifle that can be used for everything including hunting to defense to long-range shooting and the list goes on. Ruger GSR Ruger GSR is based on the Ruger M77 Hawkeye and uses an easy Mauser-style action. The capacity is 3-10 rounds based what magazine you are using.

Ruger Mini-14

If you're looking for a semiautomatic rifle with 5.56x45mm NATO but with a manual of arms that's closer to the AK-47 as opposed to the AR-15 You should take a closer look at Ruger Mini-14. Ruger Mini-14.

A great option to replace the AR-15 Mini-14 is a great alternative to the AR-15, the Mini-14 is essentially the M1 Carbine on the outside. It can hold 20 rounds, which is a typical.

Springfield M1A

M1A M1A is a real battlefield rifle. Or at the very least its select-fire model, that the M14 is. Semi-automatic .308 rifle the M1A is a fantastic option for long-distance shooting as well as for large game hunting and tactical applications. One can argue used to argue for the .308 semi-automatic gun can be described as the best multi-purpose gun that you can buy, since it can be used for for tactical and hunting purposes.

The M1A is available in three distinct sizes The standard size as well as the scout squad and the SOCOM with the 22-inch, 18-inch as well as 16 inches barrel lengths.

Conclusion

The list isn't exhaustive, but it will give an idea of the various choices available for the survival rifle.

From semi-autos to bolt actions to lever actions, the possibilities are limitless and there are numerous models and brands to pick from.

It all comes to deciding your preferences and what your requirements are. If you're looking for an all-purpose survival weapon to keep, or a gun you'd employ in a SHTF situation, then any of these options will work.

What if you could only have Only One Out Gun? Out Gun?

If you had to be forced out of your home during a time of crisis in the present, and you only had one weapon with you what weapon would you pick?

The scenario plays out like this: you have to go. If you stay, either death is inevitable If you don't leave and authorities have ordered you to leave. Therefore, you are forced to leave.

You've got your bug-out bag, your family members grab every bug out bag they have in their bags and are about to walk out of the door. The only item you'll need the gun.

The gun you carry is your primary security tool. It's the way you ensure your safety when you're vulnerable and when people who have no intention of harming you are looking to you for what you own. In simple terms without it, your odds of survival are drastically reduced.

If you're able to bug out in a vehicle or vehicle, it's easy to take several guns. It is possible to have all your bases covered in the event that you were to carry a conceal handguns, duty-sized firearm, .22 rifle, defensive rifle, hunting rifle shotgun, and so on.

However, if you must take it on foot, you'll not be capable of bringing all these guns. You'll only be able to bring one and would you like to know what the gun is?

A semi-automatic 9mm pistol that has the capacity to hold 12-rounds or more (you'll be restricted to ten rounds if you reside within one of the most restricting states or jurisdictions).

Let's look at the reason why a 9mm semiautomatic pistol is the ideal choice as gun if you're looking to get out on feet.

In the first place, it is recommended to use an assault weapon instead of the rifle or shotgun to get out on foot, for an crucial reason: it's concealable.

This is a great benefit. Being able to walk around with a rifle or shotgun on your shoulder will draw a lot of attention that is not needed, and not just from criminals or any other person who could hurt you, but from law enforcement officials as well as military service members. The capability of concealing weapons in the event of an SHTF scenario cannot be missed.

So you can say that a pistol is the ideal option for a bug-out weapon, as it is able to be hidden. Why 9mm?

The answer is simple: 9mm is the most abundant caliber available which is why it will be the easiest to locate in the midst of an incident in the event that ammo sources are completely cut off. It's inexpensive and abundant. In the moment of this writing, it's extremely easy to find a set comprising 50 FMJ rounds for less than 10 bucks this is by far the most affordable you'll find for centerfire handgun ammo.

Additionally, 9mm is an extremely effective self-defense caliber If you choose the right ammo. FMJ rounds? Ideal for training and shooters who want to have fun at the range but not for self-defense. To defend yourself, you'll need JHP self-defense ammunition like Federal HST and Hornady Critical Defense.

Why do you need do you need more than 12 rounds inside the gun at minimum? Since you might be confronted by multiple adversaries and in that the more bullets will be preferred.

There's a simple rule is essential to understand about guns: the more rounds that you have in your gun and the more time you'll have to fight.

Yes you can refill your gun, and you shouldn't leave your home without having spare magazines or ammunition for your gun at hand.

There are many circumstances that can be addressed by a larger capacity magazine versus smaller magazines. Take a look at the Glock 19, which has 15 rounds, and a Glock 43 which has just 6 rounds. There are many different risky situations that you can solve by using 15 rounds, but even do it with just 6 rounds!

The most important thing is to choose the gun you're comfortable with. If you're better at using smaller-sized guns with lesser capacity, then it's best to choose a firearm that you're not comfortable with.

But, capacity in magazines means quite a bit. Consider the scenario if you had two to four adversaries following you. Do you prefer 6-8 rounds of ammunition in a compact pistol, or 15-17 rounds in a full large firearm for duty? Exactly.

It's true that guns have their limitations. It's not the most ideal choice to hunt in any way imagination, but 9mm can be utilized to hunt smaller game or for deer, if you strike it in the critical areas and at reasonable distances.

Pistols are weak and do not do as many destruction as calibers for rifles, making them less effective for self-defense. Furthermore their range is generally less extensive.

However, the benefits of carrying a pistol as your sole gun to use in an emergency outweigh the drawbacks. Its ability to be concealed on your body is a better option as opposed to a rifle or shotgun.

Consider whether you're willing to go on the run especially in a city-based and heavily urbanized area, specifically, with an AR-15 or shotgun. It's extremely difficult to conceal, despite the many advantages it has over handguns.

With your gun is a simple matter to put it in the waistband of your jacket or shirt whenever you need to. You won't draw unnecessary interest to your self, however you're not completely at risk also.

Also, if you decide to want to go bug-out in your car take other guns like a shotgun and rifle as well. If you must get out on the ground, a pistol is the most suitable bug-out gun.

Chapter 9: The Top 10 Emp Faults To Avoid

First Mistake: You Do Not Know What an EMP Attack Is.

The first mistake that you could make while planning in preparation for EMP attack, isn't comprehending what is an EMP attack is all about in the beginning.

EMP is an acronym that stands in for electromagnetic pulse. It's a short and easy explosion of electromagnetic energy which is produced by electrically charged particles being rapidly exaggerated.

This is why EMP attacks can cause massive damage on electronic devices and some physical objects also, such as power lines.

Three specific things can trigger an EMP to occur:

It's an EMP weapon that is detonated
- A Lightning Strike
- A Natural Solar Storm

Of these three The first one is the one our enemies could attack us with. The greater the EMP could be released into space, the greater the area it will affect transformers.

They will short out, the power grid would collapse as well as a myriad of other types of devices that require electricity are not able to function.

It is a general rule the fact that an EMP always stays within the line of sight. This means that it is able to technically spread over thousands of miles if it's released at a sufficient height into the space.

The majority of nuclear weapons aren't designed to be used at high altitudes since a nuclear explosion at a high altitude would be of little use to target areas of attack.

The opposite applies to an EMP. Although the power of the released EMP could decrease with the number of miles the EMP traveled, it could cause damage to electronics for thousands, if not hundreds of miles.

It is precisely for this the reason why the threat of an EMP attack is among the biggest threats we, as a nation, face in the present. If an EMP was to explode at an altitude that was sufficient it could deliver the nation with a devastating blow that could impact our army, our government and even the everyday citizen.

The following items wouldn't be able to stand up to the force of an EMP attack:

Computer Monitors
- Desktop Computers
- Laptop Computers
Power Plants
Tablets
- Smart Phone
Cell phones
- Telephones
-- Cell Service Towers
- Automobile Engine Computers
Routers
Air Traffic Control Systems – Air Traffic Control Systems
Thermostats
-- Jet Aircraft Systems
- TV's
- Refrigerators
Internet Servers
-- Diagnostic Machines in Hospitals
-- Electronic Banking Systems

This conversation leads us to the next crucial EMP error You don't know the severity of an EMP attack can be.

Second Mistake: You Don't know how bad an EMP-related Attack Could Be

The impact that result from an EMP attack on America United States can be divided into immediate, short-term and long term consequences.

The first and foremost reason is that the first thing to consider is that an EMP attack is among the most catastrophic events that could occur for people in the United States. The reason for this is that it's a major catastrophe that could affect the entire nation in one go.

Here's what's going to happen in the immediate aftermath of any EMP attack:

The lights are out in a flash
- Every electronic device listed in the previous chapter will be shut down completely
Trains can be able to derail
All types that are public transport will stop
Cars can stall and crash into the road

Aircrafts will begin to fall from the sky
- Elevators may be stuck
Here are the short-term results from this EMP attack:
There will be no running water in the future, since water requires electricity
In the event of transformers exploding and cars and planes colliding in uncontrolled fires, they will soon begin and ravage the United States
ATM banks will stop functioning
The banks will close (you cannot access your funds)
The gas stations will stop working
The grocery stores and restaurants will close
Food that is perishable will start to spoil
You can no longer have the luxury of basic services
Here are the long-term effects the EMP attack could have:
People begin to die from starvation or dehydration.
Hundreds of suicides are expected.
People will turn on one another like savages in search of food

Violence is expected to erupt throughout the country.
Cities will be overrun by looting and riots
The supply chain could be closed as trucks cannot longer operate.
The economy will fall and the paper dollar will become ineffective
- The world will fall into chaos
- Law enforcement and the government will not be able stop the chaos
Martial law is likely to be declared
Third Mistake: You Don't Be aware of the various types of EMP Attacks
There are three types of EMP attack that can occur.
The most common type that EMP attack that is possible is known as the E1 attack. This is the fastest, and most damaging kind of EMP attack. It could last for less than a microsecond.
This kind of EMP attack that would occur in the event that an EMP weapon was to be exploded in the air.
The other type that is an EMP attack is known as the E2 attack. It is a more slow type of attack than E1 and, in actual it is

likely not originate from an explosive EMP weapon.

In reality the case, the E2 strike could occur as a result of lightning strikes. It is, in fact, the most straightforward type of EMP that can protect you and your electronic devices.

The third kind that is an EMP attack is known as the E3 attack. It's the type that is an EMP strike that could result due to the solar flare. It's also one of the fastest types of EMP strike and it could take many days (or hours at most).

The 4th mistake Then You Think EMP attacks will be Soon Over

Do you really believe that the consequences caused by an EMP attack are temporary? If so, you're seriously misinformed.

The EMP attack itself will be swift and will be over in a flash. It's the aftermath of an EMP attack that's the most tragic.

It is the case that the United States government currently has no contingency plan for what to do in case of the event of an EMP attack. That means you're completely on your own and also that the recovery time will be extremely, very long.

From the most optimistic forecasts according to the most optimistic projections, it is likely that the United States would never fully recover from an EMP attack for more than one decade, possibly even more.

That means you is never the same after one EMP attack:

There is no longer running water at your house.

You will no longer have power.

Your laptop, tablet, or phones be functioning. You'll be unable to connect with anyone.

You will no longer have cash in the bank, or have access to it.

There is no need to visit the supermarket store. There is no need to dine out in a restaurant.

You won't be able to purchase any item using paper money because the value of money will plummet in the event of a collapse in the economy (more on this in the future).

You will no longer be in a position to drive your car (more on this in the future also).

There is no longer a guarantee that you are secure in your home. The robbers, burglars, and marauders and even organising raiding parties will be on the move targeting homes and weak people.

You no longer have to be taking a drive to work or dropping off your children at school.

You will no longer live in peace within your community. In fact your neighborhood and town will soon be transformed into an area of war due to individuals turning against each other and the declaration of martial law.

The information I've provided in the previous paragraphs is what will happen to you for TEN years at the very least.

Are you able to see the reasons why you can see why EMP attack could be the most devastating catastrophe that could ever befall our United States?

This is not only an extremely tragic and awful tragedy, but it's also an extremely long-term one. It's one that's likely to transform your life completely.

In fact, in the first year following one EMP attack, nearly 90 percent of Americans will die.

5. You don't Know How to React To An EMP Attack

Let's discuss what you must immediately after the occurrence of an EMP attack (as in the moments and hours following the EMP occurred).

When you are aware you've had the EMP attack has occurred it is time to implement your plan of action into place and then follow these steps right away:

1. Make sure you are home, and that everyone in your family at home. There should be a pre-determined meeting point where each member of your family will gather at prior to when you leave to home.

2. Now is the time to begin gathering information. First is it absolutely certain that an EMP attack has actually occurred? The most reliable way to confirm is to examine a device that's not tied to the grid

power, however, it is still susceptible for an EMP. Battery powered devices work just like your smartphone. If your phone doesn't turn back on, and automobiles and electronic devices around you don't work and you can tell that there's an EMP attack has occurred.

3. The bathtubs in your home with water while there's water running. For each gallon of water you take in, cleanse it using eight drops Clorox bleach. Every gallon counts, so keep that in mind that it may likely be life-saving.

4. Now is the time to begin making use of all the money you have. You'll not have access to cash in your bankaccount, but you'll probably have an emergency cash fund at home. Because the stores will be filled with thieves soon, and the paper money will eventually become useless Use it! Visit a supermarket and tell the manager that you would like to pay for food and other items in cash and not require change. Make this decision quickly, as each and every grocery store will be

completely empty within three days, if not sooner.

5. Use a hand crank or solar radio to start listening to NOAA Weather frequencies.

6. Get your friends together. You all agree that you need to cooperate to be able to live. Collect the skills of each person you meet and assign them one of the roles below:

* Security/Neighborhood Watch
*Mechanics
* Gardeners
* Cooks
* Doctors and nurses
* Handymen
* Experts in Firearms
* Craftsmen
* Writers
* Sewers/Clothing Menders

7. Start preparing to defend the interior of your house from the intruders and raiders. The ideal is that all of your doors to the to the outside are made of steel, and your windows are made of Plexiglas. Install defensive fortifications using whatever you have available: fencing made of

barbed wire nails, bags of sand and others. Put guns and rifles in view through windows. Your home should appear as secure as you can so that nobody will feel terrified to try to steal it.

8. Secure a gun to your hip whenever you need to. A concealed carry is preferred over open carry however. Maintain your primary defensive weapon (semi-automatic shotgun, rifle, or both) easily accessible.

No mistake #6: Do Not Need to Purchase An EMP-Proofed Vehicle

The vast majority of vehicles that were manufactured in the years after 1990, will soon be ineffective following the event of an EMP attack. They'll basically be stationary shelters, and that's all it takes.

It is a good thing that you get a car that can keep working following an EMP attack, as long as you are aware of what to look out for.

The benefit of having a functioning vehicle in the event of the occurrence of an EMP incident is the fact that you are able to evacuate your residence quickly to a safe place if needed.

The downside of owning a functioning vehicle is that you'll be an obvious target in your back because you'll be one of the few vehicles that is still operating. Even if no one else will attempt to forcefully remove it away from you however, the government might attempt to seize it.

If you do decide that you'd like to have a functional vehicle after the occurrence of an EMP attack (it is best having the choice at the very minimum) it is important to be aware of what you should look for , and also particular years, models and models of cars that might be suitable for you.

Here's a list characteristics that an EMP security vehicle must possess and that includes:

AWD or 4WD

- Be Sure to Have plenty of Cargo Storage Space for Supplies
- Be Able to Carry Every Family member
- Reliable and easy to maintain

Have A Very Limited Quantity of Electronic and Computer Parts

- Have A High Towing Capacity
- Have a strong off road Capability
Get a Good Fuel Mileage
Have A Huge capacity for fuel
What are the best vehicles that can meet these characteristics while still capable of running following having an EMP attack?
Here's a list of cars that can best suit your needs:
The aforementioned Toyota Land Cruiser J40 (1960-1984)
- Toyota Hilux (before 1985)
-- Land Rover (before 1989)
• Jeep CJ5 (1979 and earlier)
- Chevrolet Blazer (before 1894)
-- Volkswagen Beetle (before 1972)
- Ford Bronco (before 1983)

No, you don't Create A Faraday Cage To Guard Your Electronic Equipment

An EMP attack can erase all of your electronic devices. But, it won't take out your electronic items that you keep inside a sturdy Faraday cage.

An faraday enclosure is an easy cage that protects electronic devices from an electric surge. It was named after the

British scientist called Michael Faraday who lived in the beginning of the 1800s.

You can also construct an affordable Faraday cage with the help of items you already have at your home.

The construction of a Faraday cage easy and should be a matter of about five minutes.

This is what you will need to know. The first step is to put together the following items:

- Cardboard Box
- T-Shirt

Wrapping with plastic Wrapping

Aluminium Foil (Heavy Duty)

Electronic Item

You just must adhere to these instructions:

1. Insulate your electronic gadget inside the T-shirt
2. Two layers of plastic wrap around the bundle of T-shirts
3. Put the wrapped package inside the cardboard box.
4. Close the cardboard box.
5. Cover three pieces of aluminum foil over the box.

Easy enough, right? Yes, your device is fully safe from EMP attack if you followed the instructions above in a proper manner.

If I was you, I'd make a few kinds of Faraday cages now (and adding electronic devices to them). The EMP attack is likely to occur sooner than later.

Make a Mistake #8: You don't Make The Required Equipment for Survival Gear You'll Will Need

As you would plan for any other catastrophe, preparing in case of an EMP attack will require you to put together all the survival equipment you'll need to endure the long-term effects of an EMP attack.

This chapter we'll dissect the different categories of survival items , and give you a list of each item that you'll need to stockpile in each category.

* Appliances that are not electrical
* Solar Oven
* Can opener for P38
* Hand-Powered Water Pump
* Meat Grinder
* Grain Grinder

* Light
*Maglite Flashlight (protected by Faraday cage)
* Batteries for spare D-cells
* Oil Lamp
* Communication Equipment
* 2 Walkie-Talkies (protect in Faraday cage)
* CB Radio
* HAM Radio
* Water and food
1. Gallon Of Water Per Person , Per Day
* Beans
The canned meat and vegetables
* White Rice
* Cereal
* Coffee
* Dried Corn
* Cornmeal
* MRE's
Honey
* Flour
* Sugar
* Salt, and Pepper
* Nuts
* Pasta

* Peanut Butter
* Powdered Milk
*Water Filter (personal)
*Water Filter (purification)
* Tablets for Water Purification
* Fire
* Matches
* BIC Lighters
* Magnesium Flint Strikers
* Cotton Balls/Q-Tips
* Vaseline
* Kindling
* Shelter
* Tarps
* Ponchos
* Garbage Bags
* String
* Rope
* Paracord
* Ground Cloth
* Personal Hygiene
* Baking Soda
* Toilet Paper
* Soap Bars
* Shampoo
* Deodorant

* Essential Oils
* Feminine Hygiene Products
* Laundry Detergent
* Dishwashing soap
* Chap Stick
* Nail Clippers
* Hand Sanitizer
* First Aid
* Antibiotics
* Prescription medications (arguably the most crucial)
* CAT Tourniquet
* Tylenol
* Ibuprofen
* Bandages in varying dimensions
* Gauze pads in different dimensions
* Butterfly Bandages
* Antiseptic Wipes
* Scissors
* Rubbing Alcohol
* Sunscreen
* Cotton Swabs
* Tweezers
* Nail Clippers
* Thermometer
* Cold Packs

* Warm Packs
* Gauze Rolls
* Epsom Salt
* Mouthwash
*Splinter Removal Kit
* Vitamins
* Neosporin
*Sterile Pads (non-stick)
* Nasal Spray
*Bug Bite Kit
* Snake Bite Kit
* Weapons
* Folding Tactical Knife
* Knife KA-BAR
* Hatchet
* Hand Saw
General Use Axe
* Common Ammunition Calibers
* .22 Rifle
A 20-gauge and a 12-gauge gun.
* Semi-Automatic Pistol available in 9mm Luger .40 S&W, or .45 ACP
Semi-Automatic Rifle available with a size of 5.56x45mm NATO or 7.62x39mm
* Rifle with Bolt Action .308 Winchester or .30-06 Springfield

The 9th Mistake: You don't know the most dangerous places to be during an EMP Attack

Following and during after an EMP attack there are certain areas you'll definitely not would like to be.

One of them is a hospital. This is especially when you are in an ICU that requires breathing tubes to maintain your life. All of these medical devices will stop working right away following the EMP attack. In addition the entire hospital will be in chaos.

Another place you'll be avoiding is the subway. Since every subway device requires electricity to function, it will be shut down immediately following an EMP attack. This means that thousands of people could be stuck in subways immediately.

The next thing to avoid is when you are on a boat in the ocean. Boats also require electricity to function and, if they are within the reach of an EMP blast, they'll become inoperable. Even if you're as just ten miles from the coast, regardless of whether you get to shore or remain stranded on the shoreline will depend on the tide.

Another area you don't wish to be in at the time of the time of an EMP attack is in an aircraft. If an EMP is activated when you're on an airplane, pray an oath, for you'll be crashing. Certain military aircrafts do provide some protection against EMPs from solar radiation, however, civilian jet airliners don't. If these aircrafts fall from the sky, the lives of millions on the ground as well as in the air will be destroyed instantly. It's as if bombs falling from the sky.

Another place you should not choose to be in during the event of an EMP strike is the middle of a tunnel. After your car's power shuts off, it's quite easy to smash into the wall or other vehicles, particularly since it will be difficult to discern where you're traveling.

The 10th error: Do Not Invest in Bartering Items to trade following the EMP Attack

When the economy is wiped out in the wake of the EMP attack, you'll no longer be able buy or sell anything with the money you have printed.

Instead, you'll only be able buy and sell items by bartering or trading with others. When you start to get low on something the only way you will be able to get more of it is to barter the item with another.

The new currency will be a common item that we now are used to.

My opinion is that the most valuable 10 bartering items following an EMP attack would be (in alphabetical order): (in the alphabetical sequence):

1. Ammo (in common calibers)
2. Alcohol
3. Coffee
4. Condoms (or birth control in general)
5. Food
6. Gasoline (or fuel in general)
7. Seeds
8. Spices
9. Toilet Paper
10. Water

Other items that are certain to become useful include:

Books

"Candy" (and sugar generally)
- Clothes
Duct Tape
- Fire Starting Devices
- Fishing Equipment
Games
Gold
- Paper
Paracord
- Pepper Spray
Rope
Sewing Kits and Knitting Kits
Silver
Sleeping Bags - Sleeping Bags
Tarps/Plastic Sheeting
Writing Utensils

Chapter 10: Hydration Packs

A popular ways to carry water on outings these days is via water bottles, like those from Camelbak canteens.

The hydration packs are big bladders, which are placed inside a compact to mid-sized backpack. It comes with a tube as well as a drinking valve that permits users to drink water throughout your travels.

This is indeed an excellent way to carry water , and it helps you keep hydrated even while in motion.

But, this isn't the method I would suggest to transport water since they're very extremely high-maintenance.

The bladder and the drinking valve and the tube in a constant state of cleanliness otherwise, mold can grow and make the drinking water unfit for consumption.

What else do you require instead?

In reality, what you require instead is a premium canteen or water bottle that you can wear on your belt or carried over your shoulder.

One of my absolute favourite drinking bottles is one of my personal favorites, the

Lifestraw water bottles. The Lifestraw is without doubt one of the top and safest water filters available on the market.

The bottle comes with the Lifestraw inside and you can refill the bottle directly from a river, stream or lake. You can drink straight from it.

Portable Generator Portable

I was uncertain on whether I should include this particular item in the checklist or not.

It is undisputed the fact that portable generators can be useful and can be found in. There is one that I use in my garage, and I would recommend that you have one too.

Generators can help maintain power for a couple of days during an outage that affects your town like. This is a situation where an electric generator could be beneficial.

For a real SHTF-related item, I consider portable generators to be a bit underrated for a single reason: they could be useless.

There could be a shortage of gas in the event of an extended catastrophe, and if you've not saved enough fuel to run your generator each day for at least six months then what value will your generator provide you?

The math is that a portable generator could use anything from ten to 30 gallons of gasoline per every day. It is also necessary to store six months of fuel to ensure that your portable generator will last for that long.

That means, even if all you require is ten gallons of fuel per day to run your generator you'd need to use 1,800 gallons of fuel to power your generator throughout that period of time.

Do you have enough space to hold around two thousand gallons of gasoline? Most people definitely do not.

It's possible to make use of your generator occasionally however, you will require a significant amount of fuel.

Also, remember that fuel has only a short shelf life and it might not even last as long for you.

Generators are also not protected from EMP strikes or solar flares. A EMP attack could be among the most destructive attacks that could strike the United States because it would completely destroy the national electricity grid...and your generator will be only a deadweight.

What do you need instead?

What you require is an alternative source of energy.

Propane is a fantastic example of what you could utilize, as is wood if you reside in a rural region.

Space heaters, stoves and lanterns are all powered by propane.

There is also solar power, which can prove to be a reliable and effective method of heating your home.

In short, there's numerous alternatives you can pick in lieu of gasoline generators that are portable.

Drum Magazines

Do you have an AR-15 or AK-47 or a semi-automatic gun similar to the ones above?

If yes, great. It's a good thing. AR-15 and AK-47 are excellent defensive rifles to keep in your arsenal as they're the best types of guns you can have to protect your home and your belongings from many adversaries when you are in the event of an SHTF scenario.

The last item you should purchase for your gun is a 100-round drum magazine. It's a cost-cutting measure and can cause you to be less effective during a battle.

The reason is that drum magazines are heavyand difficult to transport, and the majority times, they are ineffective and lead to malfunctions.

What else do you require instead?

It's easy, choose the standard 20 or 30 round box that are lightweight and simple to carry and refill, and are stable and durable.

Body Armor

It could be something you'll need. The right body armor will stop shots and fight, reduce the risk of dying if injured.

It is because of this that a lot of people believe that body armor is an excellent investment in the event of the eventual SHTF scenario.

In reality, however it is heavy and can slow the pace of your life. It can make people feel invincible , but in reality you're not. This false sense of self-confidence can be the cause of your death during a gunfight.

What You Really Need (To Take Care of) Instead

My personal opinion is to stay clear of the gunfight at all cost in the event of an SHTF situation. The last thing you must do is to walk around in all the body armor and tactical gear.

Keep in mind that body armor doesn't have to be worn for survival in an encounter with a gun. The most important thing is your ability and experience with your firearms.

Camouflage

Camouflage isn't something I would put on in a survival or SHTF scenario , as it attracts the attention of.

If you come across someone wearing an camouflage outfit It is an indication that they're likely to be interested in tactical activities, may be former military personnel, and almost definitely are carrying guns.

Wearing camouflage indicates to law enforcement officers that there is a possibility of a crime as well as to others that you may have possessions worth a lot of money.

The use of camouflage has its uses. It's useful when on the trail looking at supplies and needing to be at a distance, for example.

However, camouflage is definitely not something you'll wish to wear casually.

What Do You Need Instead

What you must instead of is wearing clothes that don't make a statement and is more subtle.

Avoid camouflage and black and stay clear of bright colors like orange, red yellow, or pink.

Colors I would recommend in the event of a catastrophe include:

Brown Brown
- Dark Green
Grey - Grey
Dark Blue - Dark Blue
Night Vision Goggles

Night vision goggles offer one benefit: they can help you see at night.

Beyond that night vision goggles are extremely expensive and require other expensive equipment like glasses, IR lasers, and helmets, to mention some of the things.

Night vision goggles are expensive, costing thousands of dollars for each set. If they cost lower than that, say about $500 or less then they'd be more popular.

Instead, you could anticipate spending anywhere from the equivalent of $3,000-$10,000 for a top-quality evening vision glasses. Sorry, but that's simply not worth it.

What Do You Need Instead

The best option for night vision glasses, in truth is flashlights. True, they reveal your location however they also allow you to see even in the dark.

My most preferred model of lightbulb is Maglite that are robust and top of the line and are also able to double as weapons for defense or clubs.

Bed Bags (For Bug Out Bags)

Sleeping bags are ideal for hunting, camping and RV road trips and more.

Do you want to find out which sleeping bags are not suitable for?

Bags for bug outs as well as survival kit.

It is because sleeping bags are massive heavy, bulky, and heavy. They will be a huge burden and take up lots of space and space inside bags for bug out and that's just not worth the expense.

What Do You Need Instead

The best option for sleeping bags in the bug-out bag would include emergency bivvies. Although they're lighter and warmer they can be folded up more compactly and are simple to transport and move around. They might not be the best option for winter time in mountain areas, however for other seasons they'll be just fine.

Tent

Similar to the sleeping bags or tents, they are absolutely no space in the bug-out bag. Neither does a survival kit.

They just consume too much space and space. One tent can weigh up to 10 pounds of weight to your bug-out bag, and that's not even counting the space it's likely to fill up.

What Do You Need Instead

What you'll require instead of the shelter is an apron, and paracord, so you can make the shelter of your choice.

It is also advisable to make the effort to learn how to construct shelters using natural resources. The forest will supply all the materials you require to build a lean-to the teepee or an A-Frame.

A paracord and tarp are each lighter than a tent and both are able to improve the security the shelter.

Chapter 11: Water

Food is essential to maintain energy, however, you can endure a long time without it. Water is more valuable and can be difficult to live without for more than three days, and within a single day, you'll feel the devastation of dehydration. In this regard it is possible that there is no thing as vital to look to find a source of water that is clean. It is necessary to drink water for cleaning, as well as for cooking food.

There won't be any running water after an EMP attack, in the sense of what we're accustomed to receiving from sinks, bathtubs, refrigerators and the like. There is still the possibility of obtaining water from rain, streams, or in some cases, even on the ground. But none of these sources can be considered a reliable sources of water. You must make sure you have the most water you can. The main questions to ask yourself are how much water you have in your storage and how you conserve it?

As a guideline, every person needs at minimum one gallon of water every day for drinking and personal hygiene reasons. This doesn't count water to wash or to cook with in this case, however for this particular example let's suggest that one gallon of water per day for each person is the amount you need to plan to stock up on.

A EMP attack is very likely to be a long-term disaster scenario. We're sorry, but If you're planning to prepare for a three-day or a week-long catastrophe (or even a months-long one) it is likely that you're severely unprepared. For the typical group of 4, you'd require 12 Gallons of water to survive an emergency scenario lasting three days. In a month-long situation of survival, you'd require ninety gallon.

For preparation for the possibility of an EMP attack, make sure you prepare the minimum of six months of your disaster preparedness. You'll need exactly that an amount of at least 7200 Gallons of water. It is a huge amount, which it really is. You'll require the space required to store all this water. However, most crucially, you'll require the expertise to properly store it. Water is essential for your health, however in the event of contamination, it can cause more harm than having any water at all.

There are two ways to store the seventy-two gallons water either by purchasing bulks and large quantities of bottled water, or by pouring all the water you have collected into containers for storage. The majority of preppers combine both techniques: bottled water is ideal for transportation container storage is more practical and permit you to keep more water in a smaller space.

Let's say that one quarter of your water storage is bottle water. The remainder of the water is kept in containers for storage. They must be made with non-corroding materials (a.k.a polyethylene container) and thoroughly cleaned. Avoid using containers at all cost even if they're completely clean. Also, make sure to change out all the water you drink at least every six months to avoid any chance of getting rotten.

Storage containers are available in sizes that range from 5 to 60 gallon. Label it all as cleaning, drinking as well as food prep water. Make note of the date on which the water was stored so you'll know when you should change it out.

However, no the amount of water you have stored up don't rely on just one method to get it. It is essential to obtain water via other methods in order to become completely self-sufficient. The most obvious source of water is streams, lakes, and rivers. It is acceptable to drink the water from these sources but only under a specific set of rules: 1. Avoid any source that is near a chemical contamination, 2. Beware of water that appears or smells unpleasant, 3. Beware of water that flows from animals' carcasses, feces or carcasses and 4. Boil water for 30 minutes, then purify it prior to any use no matter the reason.

You could also capture rainwater either by letting it be drained from your roof into a pipe collection or by collecting it under an Tarp. Purify and boil the water prior to using. This is purely a precautionary measure.

As we've discussed running water, the bathtubs and sinks will soon disappear. But, you are able to explore the possibilities with more water that you have by melting any ice cubes in your freezer, or you can use the water from the pool. It is best to limit all pool water for personal hygiene or cleaning water. The water must be cleaned and boiled prior to use.

Chapter 12: Cooking, Cooling, Heating And Lighting

Maintaining A Healthy Environment
Essential things like staying warm, escaping the heat, and cooking meals are all things we consider to be normal. If the power grid goes out and you lose power, you will be amazed at how dependent we are on electricity to fulfill the requirements. It is essential to have alternative sources to stay healthy.
Cooking

Vintage wood stoves like this were designed when there was no grid so they can not only heat your home and cook your food but some of them also feature wet backs which can provide you with a constant supply of hot water

It is essential to eat, and eat cold canned food every day for weeks. It will wear you out very quickly. In fact, you might even develop food fatigue. Food-related fatigue can cause havoc on the digestive system. It can cause diarrhoea nausea, stomach cramps and vomiting. It is important to modify your diet to avoid fatigue.

Food preparation is one of the simplest of your worries when power is off. A backyard fire pit and your barbecue or even a camp stove could be utilized to cook your food. You can cook soup stews, stews, or even casseroles if you have access to heat. Make sure you invest in one of the methods above to cook your food. Get cookware made from cast iron that can stand up to the heat of an open flame.

Make sure you have enough food which you can add to an enormous pot and then sit over an open flame. Freeze-dried meals are fantastic as they don't need any cooking. But, you'll require water as well as a method to warm the water.

You should purchase the manual kitchen tools also. Tools like a manual can opener, hand mixer with a manual and a hand-crank mixer can be useful when you need to mix your meal with no power. Make sure you have a percolator with you to make your morning coffee.

Cooling

It might not be an item you'd like to place on your top priority list but, hyperthermia can be exactly as risky as hypothermia. It is essential to maintain the right temperature to avoid heatstroke and heat exhaustion.

It is possible to keep your home cool or at the very least comfortable without power. It is necessary to cover all doors with blankets and curtains. Keep out the sun. Close the windows in case the outside temperature is extremely hot. There is no need for the heat to get into the home. If your basement is in use keep it in the area that is naturally cooler.

Do not cook indoors or run too many lights. You don't want to create excessive heat. Try to delegate the bulk of your chores for the late evening or early morning to prevent the risk of overheating. If your house isn't equipped with any trees or an opportunity to shade it then you might prefer sheltering in trees.

Heating

A simple wood heater like this is a great investment as it can be a great way to save money on gas or electricity if the grid works well BUT if the grid does go down it can be used to heat your home and with a little improvisation can be used to cook with and boil drinking water

The task of keeping your home warm can be greater issue as it is to keep the house cool in the event that you don't have a second energy source. Woodstoves are your best option. If the power goes back on, you'll be able to utilize your woodstove as a way to boost your heating bills. It can be used to cook food, dry out your clothes and also give you lighting. If you can invest in it and put a woodstove at home.

You can also keep snug by closing doors to the home to prevent drafts that aren't needed. If the temperature is cold, snuggle in a small room. The body warmth can keep your loved ones warm.

Protect the doors and windows with blankets or drapes. Then, roll up towels and put them on top of the doors to stop drafts. It is also possible to reduce drafts by taped over the windows, and then applying duct tape in order to keep it in position. In the event that you've got a south-facing glass window, and you see the sun shining shining you can leave it open and let the sun warm the space.

Do not use gas heaters, or install a generator in the house to try to keep warm. It can lead to CO poisoning. Candles that burn serve a dual purpose. It provides the user with light and also generates some warmth.

Lighting

Solar powered garden lights are very affordable and can be used as indoor lights. Just leave them outdoors during the day and bring them indoors at night.

In the dark for long periods of time can be a disaster for your mental health. It is essential to have lighting to cook or read from, as well as to give you the feeling of safety and security. There are many possibilities to get illumination into your home. And honestly, it's the most simple task to do in the event of an event of grid failure.

Flashlights are ideal to use while walking around the house or checking out things outdoors. Choose LEDs that use less power and are more bright overall. Be sure to have backup batteries in abundance.

Lanterns are a great alternative to illuminate an space. There are battery-powered lanterns as well as lanterns that have solar power. Solar lanterns are a superior alternative since they don't require that you keep a massive quantity of D-batteries in your home.

The emergency candles are a good alternative, however it is essential to ensure you don't let them go unattended. Make sure you have enough candle holders that can support the emergency candles. Candles in jars are sufficient but they will not produce the same amount of illumination like taper candle.

The solar lights that you can afford to install in your garden and along your path make great indoor lighting too. Put the lights out during the day , then bring them inside at the evening. This is an instance where you can use solar lighting to provide lighting source all night. There are a variety of styles, that provide more illumination than others. Look through your garden and home shop and select ones that you want to take inside.

Chapter 13: What Defense Is There Against Emp?

The consequences of an EMP will be devastating for the nation's infrastructure. Therefore, the question is what is the best means to defend against or deter the possibility of an EMP strike? As the guardians of a nation's security, institutions such as those of United States Pentagon have spent endless hours researching every contingency option to protect their nation from danger. When it comes to the possibility of an EMP attack, numerous possibilities for defense and protection of the nation have been analyzed.

However, it's not just people on the national scale who must shoulder the total responsibility. Every citizen must be taught as much as is possible about the methods of being able to survive. This chapter employs a dual method of explaining how the government and each individual citizen could be able to protect themselves from the ravages from an EMP.

Metallic Shielding

To use metallic shielding for electrical equipment it is necessary to utilize a continuous piece of shielding, such as steel or copper. Metal shields typically don't completely cover the interior , however they will likely contain tiny holes to allow for ventilation. Other materials, such as auxiliary ones, are typically used to make up for this apparent lack of security. The shielding should be around half a millimeter so that it can provide the greatest protection against the sonic pulse.

Tailored Hardening

If you are considering tailor made hardening of electrical devices to protect against a possible EMP attack initial thing to be taken into consideration is whether the equipment itself is functional if the hardening process is successful. By tailoring your hardening, you are only placing the most sensitive parts of electronic equipment in metallic cases. Knowing which element of an appliance device needs to be hardened and which components aren't is vital to keeping an EMP security within budget. Although this approach is less expensive, it hasn't proved to be as secure as full metallic shielding.

Training for the Private Sector

A lot of people have tried to say that there is no any contingency plan in relation to infrastructure in the private sector. This isn't the reality. Because the infrastructure of the private sector is at risk of being badly damaged, steps are being implemented to install powerful surge protectors that will be able to be able to withstand a lightning bolt and a lightning strike, but also generate electrical pulses. This is an important step towards the right direction, however, the surge protections not completely reliable and can easily be blown away however it is at a minimum a beginning in the process of preparing the private sector for the possibility of a catastrophic attack.

Finding and knocking out an EMP Device

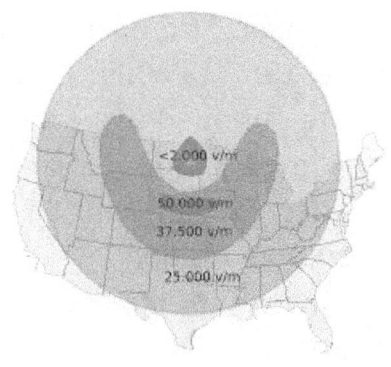

In recent times, mostly because of provocations from North Korea, the U.S. has intensified efforts to develop ways to shoot down nuclear missiles, as well as other weapons of aggression, in mid-flight. The standard strategy is to utilize offensive missiles, such as "patriot" type interceptors that shoot, aim, and then knock enemy missiles from the sky. Furthermore there are plans in development that use laser technology to destroy the targets of incoming missiles.

There is a U.S. military has prototypes of ground-based laser batteries and continuing research into space-based laser platforms , as mentioned in the Ronald Reagan's "Strategic Defense Initiative" program in the 1980's. When it comes to something more subdued like an EMP in a suitcase that terrorists are planning to use within the city, the most trusted companion could be his dog.

There are numerous programs that have trained the innate senses of the average dog to identify and locate the parts that comprise the components of an EMP device. It doesn't matter if it's patriot missiles, laser that is based on the ground or Ronald Reagan's SDI or the sniffer of your dog There are methods to find and destroy any EMP device.

Chapter 14: Finding An Emergency Heating Source

In our modern times our lives are dominated by modern technology way too often. To stay cozy and warm in the winter months, we all use an electric central heat system that comes installed in our homes or bungalows. However, the electric grid isn't so reliable as you think it is. If the power is cut off this makes electrical heating systems as well as other equipment connected to it unable to keep our homes warm.

If your gas stove is functioning you may think about heating your home. You should not use it for heating purposes. These types of equipment are not intended to provide heating and can dramatically increase the level of carbon monoxide and carbon dioxide in the air. It could cause you to become ill or trigger respiratory problems.

If you are faced with situations such as these, you can take help of the traditional methods to keep your home cozy and warm. It's time to utilize that beautiful fireplace and strive to create a warm and welcoming environment in your house. Utilize these methods to keep your home warm and cozy without electrical power.

1. Make sure to use the fireplace

There are many homes with a fireplaces that burn wood. They are mainly employed for decorative reasons since they're less efficient than central heating systems. However, in the event in an emergency, it is important to certainly get it working. Keep a few pieces of wood in your house and ensure that your fireplace is working.

It is a good idea to utilize it at minimum every month, and to keep the stock in good condition. You can buy tiny logs of wood designed for fireplaces in the market. If you don't have enough inventory, you could get together with your group of friends to cut some wood. Learn how to ignite your fireplace and using it regularly.

2. Wood-burning stove

If there isn't an existing fireplace in your home You can make a wood-burning stove for a temporary space. To build it, you'll need the stove, a few pieces of plywood, as well as the chimney pipe (with the elbow). You must place the stove near the window, with the opposite side that opens the chimney. It is possible to do this by taking out the glass panes. Utilize plywood to shut the space left in the window.

After installation and putting it in place, you can utilize the stove to create an fire, and keep the temperature of your house comfortable. In order to achieve that, it is possible to choose a variety of kinds of wood stoves are available for purchase. Choose stoves that can take wood pellets since pellets are more energy efficient, and generate more heat. But, ensure there are enough pellets that can last for a few days.

3. Heating system that uses gas catalytic technology

If you don't think you're able to accumulate wood or other kinds in fuels, certainly consider using gaz catalytic heating systems. They utilize natural gas to be their fuel source. They are constructed of ceramic bases that provide gas for burning. The combustion gas emits heat and brings warmth to the space.

It is easy to purchase several types of heaters at your local store or from any other online retailer. Additionally, you can choose the size of the heaters to fit your space. Since they do not require power, you are able to make use of them after the power goes out. In addition, you don't have to store natural gas to use them. It is simply connected to the closest station. But, they come with particular issues. They depend on the pipeline that is connected to the nearby station. If there is catastrophe, there is a chance that these lines will be damaged.

We do recommend to have at minimum one stove that is easily installed since it won't need the trouble of stock collection or installation. There's no way to tell! It could be useful in the event of a power failure and even save your life.

4. Kerosene heater

If you live in a cramped space and you don't have other option, they recommend to use a kerosene heater. They're smaller than typical fireplaces, yet are rather efficient in the way they work. Make sure to include at minimum one of these heaters in your list of necessary tools. The most appealing aspect of them is that they release warmness in all directions. This will ensure that every inch of the room receives plenty of heat.

Additionally, they don't require the installation of chimneys. Because heat doesn't go by the chimney (like fireplaces or stoves that burn wood) the heat stays to your home. This is why they are extremely efficient. But, when using them, it is important ensure that you have sufficient fuel. Without kerosene the heater is worth little or nothing. To avoid a potentially dangerous scenario, ensure you've got enough fuel.

The most important thing is to be aware that in the event of a power cut, you'll be able only to heat one room. Be sure to notify your family members of the situation and establish the hub. It is possible to use your basement as a place where all your family members can keep in touch. It is essential that all doors and walls are secured. You must make sure that your home be able to hold the amount of heat that is produced without losing a substantial portion of it.

Chapter 15: What's What Is An Emp Attack?

Electromagnetic pulses are generated through nuclear explosions. North Korea is actively threatening to test nuclear bombs, and release radiation into the air. Should North Korea tested a nuclear bomb close to the US The electromagnetic pulses could stop the entire electrical equipment in the United States. The electromagnetic pulse creates the radiation in a flash.

Scientists are of the opinion that the moment North Korea fires off a nuclear weapon, it could create to emit an electric pulse. The electromagnetic pulse may not only destroy electronic devices , but could also wipe out a large percentage of the population of the United States in one blow. We must be vigilant and secure our homes using methods of survival so that we can withstand the likely threat of attacks.

The first sign that a region or region can be affected EMP is when all electronic devices are shut down simultaneously. If a lot of electromagnetic pulses occurring simultaneously and they are physically destructive, they could cause the destruction of a lot of computers, cell phones, and other gadgets because of the sudden build-up of magnetic fields. Transformers for power would be affected in addition to causing blackouts across the nation, even in areas not specifically affected since they would be destroyed due to their connection to the exact grid.

The strength that the explosion of nuclear will be contingent on the height from which the bomb fell. The electromagnetic pulse may be very low in frequency and could also have high-intensity ultraviolet wavelengths. The US military regards the detonation of a warhead like this to be extremely risky. North Korea has threatened numerous occasions to explode this kind of warhead in the vicinity of the US. If detonated this weapon could cause death to millions of people should it be done in the correct location. It's commonly referred to as HEMP which stands for high altitude electromagnetic pulse. Furthermore it is possible that the effect of HEMP on Earth could interfere with magnetic field of the Earth, causing unknown harm over the long-term.

in the 40s. scientists realized that an electromagnet pulse was a result from a nuclear blast and that its intensity was directly related with the quantity of radiation generated. When the scientists first came up with nuclear bombs they were unable to comprehend the strength of the pulses of electricity. In 1945, Enrico Fermi anticipated the electromagnetic pulse to be strong and protected the electronics from the blast due to the fear that radiation would damage electronics.

In 1962 the nuclear tests at high altitude included high-altitude tests, and raised the consciousness of the nuclear tests conducted by the government EMPs. The general public was conscious of the importance of EMPs as years progressed. In the early 1960s the US started with the Starfish Prime project. It was a massive bomb that was located 250 miles higher than in the Pacific Ocean. The bomb was launched to show a high-altitude nuclear explosion. Starfish Prime generated electrical power all over Hawaii. It destroyed more than 300 streetlights, blocked microwaves and caused alarms to go off in burglary zones without causing physical harm to organic materials. The damage that occurred in Hawaii caused by an EMP test was quickly repaired and led to scientists becoming concerned about the effects of electromagnetic pulses. On November 22, 1962 Operation Fishbowl enabled physicists to discover the mechanical characteristics that caused electromagnetic pulses. Scientists were looking to determine the strength of the electromagnetic pulses due to the strength of Earth's magnetic field. Was it possible that electromagnetic pulses were oriented differently in higher latitudes? Scientists began to notice the repercussions of electromagnetic pulses due to the fact that microelectronics at the time were becoming more sensitive. They began a project to determine if electromagnetic pulses could pose an important issue for the US in the future.

In the early 1960s the USSR was conducting testing nuclear weapons in Kazakhstan. They were less powerful than the nuclear bombs that struck Hawaii. The Soviets were conducting tests in an area that was populated and this was highly hazardous to those living there. Kazakhstan inhabitants. Additionally that it was an area in which the magnetic field of Earth is particularly robust. The destruction that occurred in Kazakhstan is not beneficial for the country nor those who reside there. It caused the flow of electricity to swell up the power lines and a power plant to catch on fire. As there was a time when the USSR government was in the process of collapse the government, there was a collaboration between US with Russian scientists. They Russian scientists were provided with money to present their EMP expertise in a variety of scientific publications. Documentation was required to explain the EMP that took place in Kazakhstan. A portion of Kazakhstan was severely damaged by their telephone lines , despite the fact that the lines were shielded by fuses and voltage protectors that caused the EMP was able to pass through without issue.

Surge protectors can't safeguard your equipment from E1 pulses but TVS diodes will. E1 is related to the radiation gamma that is released by nuclear bombs. The electrons move at 90 percent that speed in the direction of a downward spiral. Should the field did not exist, an enormous electric current would be able to spread away from the point of the explosion. The Earth's magnetic field creates a force that causes electrons to move at an angle and deflect electrons. The result is synchrotron radiation. The gamma pulse moves at lightning speed, and directly results in a radiated electromagnetic signal. An electromagnetic pulse is generated. Scientists are currently working on questions of discovering the reason for why it is that the E1 pulse is created by nuclear weapons, and released at higher altitudes. In the year 1962, Conrad Longmire of Los Alamos National Lab provided numerical data on the E1-related pulse. Scientists in 1962 carried out an additional nuke test. The test generated normal gamma rays, and produced the energy equivalent to 2 mega-electronvolts. It is believed that the E2 explosion of nuclear warheads is result of scattered gamma-rays and inelastic, gamma generated by neutrons. The E2 part is located at the center of the pulse and runs for approximately 1 microsecond to one second following an explosion in the nucleus. It is similar to lightning.

If an E1-related pulse occurs then the E2 component is followed. The E1 pulse damages devices that are normally protected against E2. The technical aspect of E2 alone is thought as the most straightforward to guard against. If it occurs following the E1 pulse, there is no way to stop it. We have defensive measures to be prepared and defend against lightning strikes however, we don't have any protection against the effects of an E1 blast.

In 2004 in 2004, the US Electromagnetic Pulse Commission announced that the issue was with the infrastructure of the country. The infrastructures are protected by measures to guard against lightning strikes, however they aren't protected from E1. The E2 component appears a little after the initial component. This allows it to destroy surge protectors and also to damage electronic systems. It is believed that the E3 element is an slow pulse , and creates distortion in the magnetic field of Earth. Similar to geomagnetic storms that are caused by intense Solar coronal mass-ejection E3 pulses generate geomagnetically induced currents that may damage electric components like powerline transformers.

Chapter 16: Solar Panels The Most Effective Types To Make

One of the most efficient ways to make an energy source that is self-sustaining is to make use of solar panels. They transform the energy from the sun into energy.

But, it is important to note that there are many different types of solar panel. Not all can be made in the same way, since there are a variety of solar panels on the market and you'll need be mindful of.

Two of the most popular types of solar panels are the monocrystaline solar panel and the amorphus and they're the two types of solar panels we'll be discussing today. We'll look at the particulars of each, and look into the advantages and disadvantages of each.

Let's begin with the Amorphus solar panels:

Amorphus Solar Panels

Amorphus solar panel are called thin film solar panels. They're named that way due to the technology they utilize is totally distinct from monocrystaline panels, and even different varieties of solar panels like the polycrystalline.

Amorphus solar panel is an older technology that is not likely to be mature until at least a decade has passed, since the technology must remain in development.

In essence, solar panels made of amorphus are made of photovoltaic components which are placed on an unglazed solid surface. Amorphus is only one type of a photovoltaic substance which is utilized. Others include copper indium galllium selenide and cadmium tellinguride.

How do Amorphus solar panels, also known as thin-film solar panels in general perform? Let's just declare that they are not very efficient in energy efficiency compared with other solar panels. In fact, are generally regarded as being among the worst types of solar panels that are available.

However, on the other hand of the coin, amorphus solar panels are among the least expensive varieties of solar panels you can purchase. This is due to the fact that the materials used to make these panels are also inexpensive which is the reason their efficiency in energy of 7 to 13 percent is so low.

However the efficiency of energy use for Amorphus solar panels (as as the thin film solar panels generally) is predicted to improve in the coming years as technology advances. It's not a stretch to think that we'll soon achieve energy levels of 15 percent or more using the amorphus solar panels.

In sum, the benefits of amorphus as well as thin film solar panels are:

They are extremely affordable and simple to make in mass production

They're among the most efficient solar panels home owners and preppers can purchase

The temperature of high temperatures has less impact upon their general performance contrast to other varieties of solar panels.

The disadvantages of Amorphus solar panels are that they can be a bit expensive.

They are more energy efficient compared to other solar panels due to their lower price and less expensive materials that are used (rates typically drop by 10 percent or less).

Amorphus solar panels tend to degrade more quickly than better quality and higher cost types of solar panels.

The technology to make solar panels with thin films is just beginning to mature, but the technology is developing.

In essence, amorphus solar panels are a fantastic solar panel in the event that money is an issue and you want to make your expenditure as low as you can.

If you're willing to pay more for an energy-efficient product You have other options, like those...

Monocrystalline Solar Panels

In all the types of solar panels that are available monocrystalline solar panels represent the oldest and the most mature technology.

Like the name suggests, the monocrystalline panels of solar are constructed with a single silicon crystal structure. The solar cells on the panel will be identical colors.

One of the greatest advantages of Monocrystalline solar panels lies in they're the highest efficient of any solar panel available.

With efficiency ratings typically around twenty percent or more and they are able to provide more than more power of the solar panels made of amorphus as we have previously discussed. They're also efficient in energy usage to the point where they will continue to harvest energy and supply power to your home even under poor lighting conditions. This is an enormous benefit on cloudsy days.

Additionally, monocrysstalline solar panels provide the longest lifespan of solar panel prior to the time they need to be replaced. The majority of panels lasting for twenty-five years or more at a minimum.

However, monocrystalline solar panels are also extremely expensive, and you're paying for a high-end product. If budget isn't a concern it's the best solar panel for you for you, however when you're looking for a low-cost option, you'll be unable to find a better option.

Additionally, it's crucial to know of the fact that panels with monocrystalline silicon aren't the most reliable option in harsh weather conditions, and is a real trouble.

They are very effective of capturing the sunlight's energy in low-light and cloudy conditions. However, when they are exposed to the elements of dirt, rain or snow, they can begin to have issues and their efficiency decrease.

This is why you'll be required to protect your monocrystalline solar panels by using things like tarps times when the weather turns bad. It's definitely a pain, but there's a trade-off for everything, isn't there?

Monocrystalline solar panels have many advantages. These are:

They are the most energy-efficient type of solar panel available on marketplace, with prices generally exceeding 20% or higher (up to more than four times as much power as the amorphus solar panels)

They use the most ancient and most advanced technology in any solar panel

They offer the longest life span and the majority of manufacturers in monocrystalline solar panel granting warranties of twenty-five years or more
They do well in dim light conditions.
Monocrystalline solar panels include:
They are extremely expensive and aren't the ideal option for people with a limited budget.
If exposed to snow, dirt or other outdoor hazards Their energy efficiency will decrease dramatically.
Solar Panel Inverters
If the power grid fails and you don't have a reliable source of power, you'll be in a bind.
This is why it's crucial to have a self-sustaining power source. The best solution is solar panels you can put on your roof, the front of your yard or even on your balcony or patio.
But using solar panels to produce electricity isn't a straightforward topic. If you're a novice to the topic it might seem like you'll need to put several panels out in the open and connect them to a power

outlet but this couldn't be further from the reality.

Alongside the solar panels in addition, you'll have to purchase an inverter solar. An inverter for solar is an electric converter that can convert the DC power that is gathered from your solar panels . It will transform it into AC power that can be used.

If you don't have the power inverter the solar panels would practically useless for you.

Just as there are various types and materials for solar panels and in the market, there are also different kinds of power inverters available as well.

The four most common kinds of power inverters are listed below, alphabetically:

Inverter Battery

Inverters for battery power used to be extremely rare, but this has changed in recent times to the point where they have seen a dramatic increase in their popularity.

A battery powered inverter requires a battery order to function (obviously). The major benefit is that it allows solar panels to function regardless of the status of your energy grid.

It means your system's solar panels will operate 100 percent, even when the power grid goes completely out of commission. There's some disagreement over the extent to which solar panels are negatively affected due to power grid outage situations like EMP attacks, however using a battery inverter you can almost guarantee you'll be able to trust that the system will continue to function.

If the power grid fails in the event of a power outage, the battery-powered power inverter needs the primary source of power that powers your solar panel to stop making electricity. This is referred to as anti-islanding which is the exact opposite of islanding in which power generated is used to run a place when there is power grid being down.

The inverter for the battery itself can monitor the power between the grid and the solar system, while keeping your batteries fully recharged. It also can monitor the battery's condition and monitor the battery's condition.

Central Inverter

If you're searching for an inverter for power capable of being able to supply energy to the most solar panels feasible, then the best alternative could include central inverters.

Central inverters perform very similarly to string inverters, and we'll talk about in a minute. In essence, central inverters are made to accommodate multiple panels at once. Instead of strings from each panel connecting through the inverter, similar to the way string panels function with string panels, in central inverters, the strings are connected as"combiner boxes.'

The combiner box was designed to supply DC power through the central inverter where it is then officially transformed into useful AC power. Therefore, it's an additional cost and an accessory you'll require however, if it's able to provide more solar panels with time, it could be the best for you.

However, in all honesty central inverters aren't required for simple RVs or homes but are more to be used for larger structures or production installations. But, it's something to be aware of.

Micro Inverter

The other alternative is micro inverters. This is becoming a more sought-after option for suburban houses and other homes for residential use.

If you're using micro inverters it is necessary to purchase an inverter to each solar panel. Inverters convert that panel's DC electricity to the AC power you can utilize right from the panel.

This is important for a important reason: If all solar panels have been connected to the exact same inverter when one of them isn't working or at best not generating the power is expected, this could affect the entire system by decreasing the overall amount of energy you're getting.

However, if you're using one inverter attached to each panel, this issue will be eliminated as is the efficiency of of the solar panels won't be affected by any means.

Another benefit of micro inverters is that they be able to monitor how each panel, allowing you to quickly recognize when an individual panel is performing poorly. Some micro inverters can be purchased alongside the panels and are already integrated by the manufacturer making them an ideal choice for installation.

Solar Inverter

The most popular type of solar inverter we'll talk about is an inverter for solar. This setup is the one you will need. you'll need to set up the solar panel in rows, or , in this instance, called stream.

If you have 15 total panels, you could choose to break them down into five "strings" comprising three panels each as an example.

There will be many strings that connect the panels to your inverter. This is why they are called a string inverter. The inverter takes all the DC energy from the solar panels simultaneously and converts it to AC power.

String inverters are certainly the most popular choice for inverter usage using solar panels, and are the most well-known alternative. This is a well-tested technology and also more affordable than micro inverters.

As was mentioned above in this setup only one bad solar panel could compromise each of them and decrease the power of your system overall. This is the main downside of this setup that you'll be faced with.

The Reasons You Are In Need Of Ham Radio Ham Radio

The phones are not working. The internet is not working. There is no way to contact the ambulances or police for assistance. The power is not on. The water isn't running.

In such a chaos, how do you connect with people who live far away? How do you connect with relatives and friends who are out from town or in another the state? What are the best ways to learn about what's happening in the world outside?

The solution is that you'll need an emergency communications device which can remain operational even when the power grid is out of service. What emergency communication device is you supposed to utilize?

There are many emergency communication options , but possibly the best of them choice is Ham radio.

Why Ham radios are the best emergency communications device for survivalists and preppers? Let's explore:

What's the reason? Ham Radio Is The Best Communications Device for Preppers in an Emergency

There are a variety of emergency communication equipment, including CB radios, GMRS radios FRS radios to walkie-talkies however, an Ham radio is perhaps the most reliable due to a variety of reasons.

The primary reason is that the first reason is that a Ham radio is extremely simple to master. It is also possible to connect with emergency services so that you'll be able to learn more about what's happening to the world outside during a disaster.

Additionally it is worth noting that Ham radios are also extremely versatile. Ham radio comes with a broad signal range and can connect to anyone in the world regardless of whether you're located in the rural or urban environment. Contrary to this other types of communications devices, like CB radios, have a restricted ranges of just a couple of miles. Walkie-talkies can reach up to forty miles or so but it's still limited.

Another benefit to using Ham radios Ham radio is that it has access to a greater spectrum of frequencies compared to other types of radios. CB radios for instance can only be used from 26 MHz up to 27 MHz.

In summary, the reason that can be persuasively to argue to the effect that the Ham radio can be described as the most suitable kind of radio for preppers are the following:

It's simple to make use of

It is a very broad variety

You are able to access more frequencies
You are able to easily reach out to the emergency service for communication
What's it like to get into Ham Radio?
A Ham radio isn't something you can simply buy and use immediately. It is rather, you need to obtain a complete licence to use.
In fact, there's an entire community who utilize Ham radios. People who wish to connect with others around the globe using wireless technology utilize them, along with emergency rescue teams and preparedness personnel.
In the present, there are around 750,000 Ham radio users within the United States alone, with more than two million worldwide.
Ham Radio Frequencies
As we mentioned previously As was mentioned previously, using Ham radios Ham radio signifies that you are able to access more frequencies compared to other radios.
Ham radios utilize frequencies that span the entire radio spectrum as allowed by

the FCC to amateurs with licenses. They can operate up to or beyond the AM broadcast, up to gigahertz, and microwave ranges, too.

If you're planning to send a signal in daylight hours the best option would be to utilize the 15 to 27 MHz band. In the evening, you'll need to decrease your range to 2 to 15 MHz to achieve the most effective results.

Getting Your Ham Radio License

As mentioned earlier that you must obtain the right license to operate the Ham radio. The three kinds of licenses required for Ham radio are: general, technician, and the extra. If you obtain one of these licenses, it is valid for 10 years, however you'll need to take a test to be eligible for it.

What is the difference between licenses from each other? In essence, they grant you to use different frequencies. The "extra license" gives you access to more licenses than the general and technician licenses, and the general is more than technicians. You'll get the idea. Consider it as intermediate, beginner and expert.

When you purchase the entry-level tech license you'll be granted access to all amateur bands that is greater than 30 MHz. The general license gives users access to bands of the amateur that are less than 30 MHz. The general license gives you access to the HF bands, which means you can converse with people hundreds, or even hundreds of kilometers away.

To become licensed to operate the Ham radio, you'll be required to pass the test with the club for amateur radio closest to where you live. The tests are typically conducted each month or quarterly during the year.

It will cost you about 20 dollars or less to pass the test. However, it will vary based on the radio station.

The test is administered by an examiner who is a volunteer who will test you on a total of thirty-five questions. To pass, you must to score at least twenty-six.

After passing, your test results and other information will be sent at the FCC. After passing, you will be granted an Ham radio licence within 2 weeks.

Conclusion

The future isn't certain and you definitely don't want to live your life looking forward to the next day However, you can take some things to ensure that your future will be a little more pleasant. After you've accumulated the perfect stash of food and water for the survival and spent the time to study gathering and purifying water, you'll feel more comfortable. You'll have peace of peace of mind knowing that regardless of the future you've done all you could to provide your family and yourself with an opportunity to fight.

A wait-and-see strategy is not the best idea. It is likely that natural disasters will take place. It's just as likely that there will be an act of civil war or tensions that impact a particular part of the globe. Because the economies of the world have a common ground, it shouldn't wait long to see the domino effect sweep across every nation and leave people scrambling to get by. Don't be caught out of the loop and not prepared to handle a disaster. Make every effort to make sure you have the basic necessities of life, so that the worst happens you don't have to worry about how you'll ensure that your family is fed and watered. Your focus can be on other essential tasks such as building shelters and rebuilding.

It's not difficult to prepare for today when the supplies are easily available. Simply, you need determination and dedication. Consider your family members and what it means to them, and then start!

www.ingramcontent.com/pod-product-compliance
Lightning Source LLC
Chambersburg PA
CBHW071840080526
44589CB00012B/1071